LITTLE-KNOWN MUSEUMS
IN AND AROUND
PARIS

LITTLE-KNOWN

MUSEUMS

IN AND AROUND

PARIS

by Rachel Kaplan

HARRY N. ABRAMS, INC., PUBLISHERS

To Alexandre,
who showed me that love and creation can go happily together

Editor: Adele Westbrook
Designer: Lorraine Ferguson

Library of Congress Cataloging-in-Publication Data
Kaplan, Rachel.
   Little-known museums in and around Paris / Rachel Kaplan.
      p.   cm.
   Includes bibliographical references (p.   ) and index.
   ISBN 0–8109–2676–8 (pbk.)
   1. Museums—France—Paris—Guidebooks. 2. Paris (France)—
   Guidebooks. I. Title.
AM48.P3K36 1996
069' .0944'36—dc20   95–52781

Front cover:
The entrance to the Cernuschi Museum, Paris

Back cover:
The second-floor gallery of The Royal Abbey of Chaalis and Its Collections,
Fontaine-Chaalis

Rachel Kaplan was educated at the Lycée Français de New York and at
Northwestern University, where she earned a B.S. in Journalism.
She is an international correspondent who has written articles for American,
British, French, and Czech publications on a wide range of subjects.

Printed and bound in Hong Kong

Harry N. Abrams, Inc.
100 Fifth Avenue
New York, N.Y. 10011
www.abramsbooks.com

CONTENTS

———◆———

Acknowledgments

I would like to express my whole-hearted gratitude to Paul Gottlieb, President and Publisher of Harry N. Abrams, Inc., for his unflagging support and encouragement of this project. I also owe a tremendous debt to my editor, Adele Westbrook—not only for her inestimable suggestions and sensitive editing, but also for her invaluable assistance throughout the creation of this book. In addition, much appreciation is due Lorraine Ferguson for the book's elegant and accessible design.

I also want to thank French photographer Matthieu Deluc for his fine photography that reveals the many splendors of these little-known museums—both inside and out—as well as for his assistance in working with each of these institutions.

It is essential to give due recognition to both Publimod'Photo labs for their superb color work and to Toros Laboratories for their stunning black-and-white custom printing. The quality of the images in this book reflects their passionate commitment to fine photography. (Unless specified otherwise, all photography in this book is by Matthieu Deluc.)

I would also like to thank the following museum curators and directors for their indispensable assistance in the creation of this book: M. Aymar de Virieu, Director, M. and Mme. Robert-Henri Bautier, Curators, Le Domaine de Chaalis; Mme. Michèle Hournon, Co-Secretary of the Association des Amis d'Alexandre Dumas; Mme. Judith Meyer-Petit, Curator, La Maison de Balzac; Mme. Brigitte

Richard, Public Relations Director, M. Etienne Féau, Curator, African Arts, M. Philippe Peltier, Curator, Oceanic Arts, Mme. Marie-France Vivier, Curator of Arts of the Maghreb, Le Musée des Arts d'Afrique et d'Océanie; M. Jean-Paul Favand, Director, Le Musée des Arts Forains; Mme. Martine Jaoul, Curator, Mme. Anne-Marie Kefi, Director of Press Relations, Le Musée des Arts et Traditions Populaires; M. Henri Bouilhet, Director, Le Musée Bouilhet-Christofle; Mme. Antoinette Fäy-Hallé, Curator, Mme. Tamara Préaud, Archivist, Le Musée National de la Céramique; M. Gilles Béguin, Curator, Le Musée Cernuschi; M. Pascal de la Vaissière, Curator, Le Musée Cognacq-Jay; Mme. Dany Sautot, Curator, Le Musée de Cristal de Baccarat; M. George Proust, Director, Le Musée de la Curiosité et de la Magie; Mme. Arlette Sérullaz, Curator, Le Musée National Eugène Delacroix; Mme. Agnès Dellanoy, Curator, Mlle. Nancy Hérault, Public Relations Director, Mme. Claire Denis, Advisor, Le Musée Départemental Maurice Denis—"Le Prieuré"; Mme. Anne Hoguet, Curator, Le Musée de l'Eventail; Mme. Dina Vierny, President, M. Olivier Lorquin, Co-director, Le Musée Maillol—Fondation Dina Vierny; Contre-Amiral François Bellec, Director, Le Musée de la Marine; Mme. Catherine Vaudour, Curator, M. Eric Delpont, Assistant Director of Collections and Exhibitions, Le Musée de l'Institut du Monde Arabe; Mme. Evelyne Cohen, Curator, Le Musée de la Monnaie; M. Jean-Marc Tarrit, Director, Le Musée de Montmartre; Mme. Geneviève Lacambre, Curator, Le Musée Gustave Moreau; Mlle. Sophie Le Tarnec, Archivist, Le Musée Nissim de Camondo; M. Claude Pigeard, Director, Le Musée de l'Outil; M. Bernard Marchois, Curator, Le Musée Edith Piaf; MM. Samy and Guido Odin, Co-directors, Le Musée de la Poupée; Mme. Claude Moreau, Le Musée Maurice Ravel; Mme. Julia Fritsch, Curator, M. Michael Erwin, Librarian, Le Musée National de la Renaissance— Le Château d'Ecouen; Mme. Ornella Volta, Curator, Le Musée Erik Satie; Mme. Anne-Marie de Brem, Curator, Le Musée de la Vie Romantique; Mme. Noëlle Chabert, Curator, Le Musée Zadkine.

On a personal note, I would also like to thank my good friends Vilma Barr, Jane Biberman, Jean-Manuel Bourgois, Jolie Cross-Doyle, Tana Hoban, Susanna Kaplan, John Morris, and Sheila Johnson Robbins for their valuable assistance and consideration.

—R.K.

Introduction

In June 1993, I made a delightful discovery on a quiet side street of the Marais in Paris. It was an extraordinary museum known as the *Musée Cognacq-Jay*—a magnificently restored private mansion that represented the residence of a wealthy French bourgeois family during the eighteenth century. Touring the museum's four floors of stunning, yet intimate rooms, filled with exquisite period furnishings and accessories, as well as paintings by such masters as Rembrandt, Chardin, Canaletto, and Watteau, I was awestruck. Much to my surprise, I learned that this jewel of a museum was rarely visited by more than a handful of people—and was not even familiar to most Parisians.

Several months later, I uncovered yet another intriguing and little-known museum (in a private apartment) dedicated to the memory of Edith Piaf. This museum could be visited only by appointment, but it was well worth making the advance arrangements.

It is a pity that such museums are not better known and more frequented, I thought, especially since many of them were at least listed in certain guidebooks and mentioned in various cultural publications. It was then that a thought occurred to me: why not create a book which, through words and images, would reveal the hidden splendors and remarkable objects to be found in these little-known museums?

By the phrase "little-known," I am referring to museums whose settings, histories, collections, and ambiance tend to be largely overlooked by the general public. Their range is extensive and surprising—encompassing museums dedicated to everything from magic, carnival art, and handmade fans, to the elaborate decorative arts of the Renaissance and eighteenth-century France. Their locales vary as well: walk-up apartments; a house once occupied by an actor in Molière's troupe; a Gallo-Roman bath built in the second century A.D. As for the objects so lovingly exhibited within these sites, I found everything from masterpieces by Giotto to an early abstract landscape painted by a Montmartre donkey! Many of these museums provide excellent self-guided tours, while the collections in others take on an added dimension through the interaction between curator and visitor. (Because so many of these museums are atypical, it is advisable to call in advance to confirm their visiting hours, as well as any special arrangements that might have to be made. It is also important to note that after October 18, 1996, all telephone numbers in the Paris region, including Paris itself, will be preceded by 01, a change that is indicated in parentheses throughout this book.)

The men and women who have either created or collaborated on the form and content of these unique museums are passionate and committed; the information they so generously furnished was always intriguing and often downright fascinating. My greatest pleasure was to find that one of the most famous and most frequented cities in the world—Paris—still had secrets, wonderful secrets, to share with us.

While working on this book, I was not only privileged to learn much that I didn't know about the art, culture, and history of Paris and its surroundings, but was also introduced to many aspects of the rest of the world, as well. *"Il n'y a rien de plus amusant que d'apprendre"* ("There is nothing more delightful than learning"), Henri Bouilhet, curator of the Christofle Museum, told me one day, and he's undoubtedly correct. I hope that the readers of this book, whether they share in my discovery of the *Little-Known Museums In and Around Paris* at home, while settled in a comfortable armchair, or have the opportunity to appreciate these wonderful treasures in person, will agree.

Map of Museum Sites In and Around Paris

(see Numerical Legend on pages 14–15)

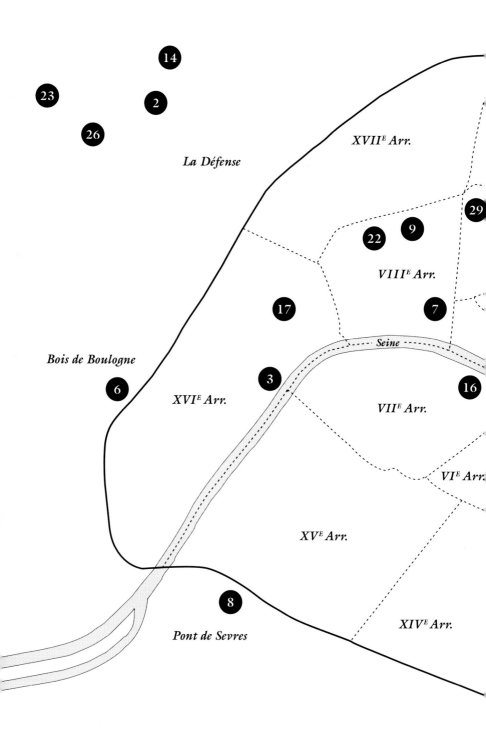

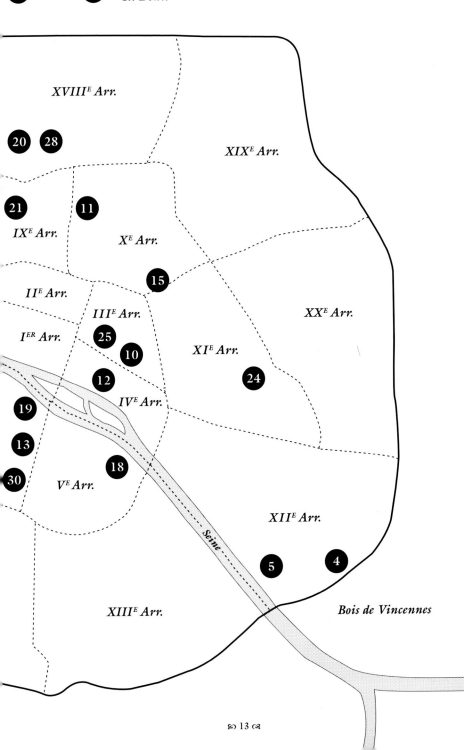

St. Denis

XVIIIE Arr.

XIXE Arr.

IXE Arr.

X^E Arr.

IIE Arr.

IIIE Arr.

IER Arr.

XXE Arr.

XIE Arr.

IVE Arr.

V^E Arr.

XIIE Arr.

Seine

XIIIE Arr.

Bois de Vincennes

Numerical Legend for Museum Sites In and Around Paris

(see Map on pages 12–13)

1 Le Domaine de Chaalis
The Royal Abbey of Chaalis and Its Collections

2 Le Domaine du Château de Monte-Cristo
The Monte-Cristo Estate and Castle

3 La Maison de Balzac
The House of Balzac

4 Le Musée des Arts d'Afrique et d'Océanie
The Museum of African and Oceanic Arts

5 Le Musée des Arts Forains
The Museum of Carnival Art

6 Le Musée des Arts et Traditions Populaires
The Museum of Popular Arts and Traditions

7 Le Musée Bouilhet-Christofle
The Bouilhet-Christofle Museum

8 Le Musée National de la Céramique
The National Museum of Ceramics

9 Le Musée Cernuschi
The Cernuschi Museum

10 Le Musée Cognacq-Jay
The Cognacq-Jay Museum

11 Le Musée de Cristal de Baccarat
The Museum of Baccarat Crystal

12 Le Musée de la Curiosité et de la Magie
The Museum of Curiosities and Magic

13 Le Musée National Eugène Delacroix
The Eugène Delacroix Museum

14 Le Musée Départemental Maurice Denis — "Le Prieuré"
The Maurice Denis Museum — "The Priory"

15 Le Musée de l'Eventail
The Fan Museum

Le Domaine de Chaalis

The Royal Abbey of Chaalis and Its Collections

**Fontaine-Chaalis
60305 Chaalis
Tel: (16) 44–54–04–02**
*(After October 18, 1996, this
phone number changes to
(03) 44–54–04–02.)*

**Open Monday through Friday
2:00 P.M. to 6:30 P.M.;
weekends and holidays from
10:30 A.M. to 12:30 P.M.
and from 2:00 P.M. to 6:30 P.M.
March 1 to November 1.
Open Sunday and holidays from
1:30 P.M. to 5:30 P.M.
November 2 to March 1.
Open year-round to groups with
reservations.**

Restaurant, tearoom with terrace.

Access:
- **By car: Forty kilometers from
Paris via the Autoroute du Nord
(A1); from Paris, exit at Survilliers-
Saint-Witz, direction Ermenonville,
then to the Mer de Sable.**

FORTY minutes by car from the tall gleaming modern towers of La Défense, one can discover the romantic ruins of the thirteenth-century Royal Abbey of Chaalis next to the forest of Ermenonville. Little is left of its Neo-Gothic edifice but for the stone remains of the northern transept and fragments from the cloister's galleries. Only the Abbey's chapel, erected by Pierre de Montreuil, architect of the Sainte-Chapelle in Paris, has been restored to its former splendor.

Saint-Louis (King Louis IX), who organized the last two Crusades, came to Chaalis to live as a monk when the Abbey was at the center of power and influence. Not only did it have a celebrated library that attracted prominent theologians and poets, it also was renowned for its fine table, which benefited from a plentiful supply of fish and game.

A VIEW OF THE ROYAL ABBEY OF CHAALIS WITH ITS WELL-PRESERVED
THIRTEENTH-CENTURY CHAPEL AND SPLENDID CHÂTEAU,
NOW THE PREMISES OF THE NÉLIE JACQUEMART-ANDRÉ MUSEUM.

AT THE END OF THE GROUND-FLOOR
GALLERY IS A PAIR OF RARE
TAPESTRY HANGINGS
ONCE OWNED BY POPE URBAN VIII
AND THE MONUMENTAL BUST OF
COSIMO DE' MEDICIS FROM THE ATELIER
OF BACCIO BANDINELLI.

THIS LENGTHY, SUN-LIT CORRIDOR
IN NÉLIE JACQUEMART-ANDRÉ'S
CHÂTEAU EXHIBITS AN EXTRAORDINARY
COLLECTION OF BUSTS
DATING FROM ANCIENT TIMES UP UNTIL
THE EIGHTEENTH CENTURY.

When Cardinal Hippolyte d'Este —son of Alphonse d'Este and Lucrezia Borgia and cousin to King Francis I—was appointed head of the Royal Abbey in the sixteenth century, he commissioned one of the greatest Renaissance painters, Niccolo dell'Abbate, the collaborator of Primaticcio at Fontainebleau, to decorate the chapel walls and vaulting with frescoes. Amazingly enough, these splendid works of art have resisted the ravages of time.

However, by the early eighteenth century, the Abbey's buildings were in dire need of renovation. The new abbott authorized that the thirteenth-century Abbey cloister be torn down and replaced by a classical building conceived by Jean Aubert, the architect who designed the Palais-Bourbon (the present Chamber of Deputies) in Paris. Unfortunately, Aubert was never able to complete his undertaking. Heavily laden with debt, the Abbey was forced into bankruptcy and liquidated in 1785.

Despite the Abbey's demise, its woodland setting was magnificent, and therefore irresistible to a buyer who envisioned transforming it into a grand country estate. That's exactly what the wealthy and socially well-connected Rose-Paméla de Vatry had in mind when she acquired the property in 1851. She not only completed the work Aubert had begun—transforming the Abbey into a sumptuous château, complete with French formal gardens and an orangery—but bought back much of the estate's 2,000 acres that had been liquidated.

In 1902, Nélie Jacquemart-André, widow of the wealthy banker Edouard André (André had also been a director of the *Gazette des Beaux-Arts* and one of the co-founders of the Musée des Arts Décoratifs), bought the estate to house the staggering collections of art, objects, and furniture she had collected on her extensive trips abroad.

If this splendid estate had a magnetic pull on Nélie Jacquemart-André, it was understandable. Despite her humble background, as a young woman she had come to know well the cloistered, privileged life at the château. The childless Madame de Vatry had developed an attachment to Nélie and often invited her for extended stays. It was in this lavishly furnished and inviting home, famed for its annual hunt banquets, that Nélie encountered the Orléans aristocracy, as well as the nobility and

THIS PORTRAIT OF NÉLIE AT TWENTY-SIX, WHEN
SHE WAS AN ART STUDENT IN ROME, WAS DONE BY HENRI REGNAULT;
IT OCCUPIES A PROMINENT POSITION IN HER BOUDOIR.

wealthy bourgeoisie of the Second Empire.

Recognizing that her protégée was a gifted artist, Madame de Vatry made it possible for Nélie to join the atelier of Léon Cogniet, frequented by women painters (who were still barred from the Ecole des Beaux-Arts). After studying painting in Italy with Ernest Hébert, the director of the Villa Medici, the talented young woman returned to Paris, where she became an accomplished society portraitist. In 1872, she painted the portrait of the man who would become her husband nine years later, Edouard André, heir to a prominent Protestant banking fortune.

Although this marriage had initially been one of convenience (the André family wanted their son, a confirmed though physically ailing bachelor, to settle down), the match turned out well, each spouse complementing the needs and interests of the other. In the years they were married, the Jacquemart-Andrés came to be known as important collectors of priceless art and furniture. When Edouard André died suddenly in 1894, Nélie inherited his entire estate and fortune, making it possible for her to travel around the world in pursuit of the rare and beautiful objects she so coveted. Part of the pleasure of a visit to the Jacquemart-André château at Chaalis is discovering how this determined and exceptional woman used her painter's eye to furnish and decorate a home that would someday become a museum.

By the time she had acquired the estate, Madame Jacquemart-André had amassed an awesome collection of rare eighteenth-century French furniture, ancient Roman, Medieval, and Renaissance statuary, as well as hundreds of paintings, drawings, and engravings from the Renaissance to the eighteenth century. Nor was that all. Her travels to Egypt had yielded some remarkable archaeological

THE GORGEOUS "INDIAN ROOM" IS FURNISHED WITH RARE CARPETS FROM CAIRO AND SILVER-EMBOSSED CHAIRS, AS WELL AS DISPLAYS OF UNUSUAL ARMS AND ARMOR. IT WAS HERE THAT NÉLIE RECEIVED THE MAHARAJA OF KAPURTHALA IN 1902.

THE DINING ROOM AT CHAALIS WAS THE SETTING FOR ELEGANT DINNERS ATTENDED BY MEMBERS
OF THE FRENCH NOBILITY AND THE WEALTHY BOURGEOISIE OF THE BELLE EPOQUE.
IT CONTAINS FOUR LARGE ANIMAL PAINTINGS—
TWO BY ALEXANDRE FRANCOIS DESPORTES AND TWO BY JEAN-BAPTISTE OUDRY.

finds, while her journeys through India and Burma in 1902 had led to acquisitions of precious furniture, as well as Oriental carpets and objects from Buddhist temples.

Nowhere is her dazzling penchant for collecting more evident than in the room once reserved for hunt banquets. Known as the "Monk's Room," its cavernous size is over-shadowed by an enormous fireplace whose mantel is ornamented by a life-size carved stag. Among the antiquities and rare artwork in this one room are thirteenth-century jewel and enamel-encrusted crosiers from the ancient Abbey of Chaalis, ornate Renaissance furniture, and two panels by Giotto, one of Saint John

the Baptist, the other of Saint Laurence, executed for a polyptych in the Chapel of Pulci-Berardi for the Church of Santa Croce in Florence.

The grandiose downstairs gallery conceived by Jean Aubert contains an impressive parade of antique marble busts, dating from ancient Rome to the eighteenth century, as well as glass cabinets filled with hundreds of small amulets, religious relics, and ancient objects.

While the château boasts an elegant *grand salon* with seventeenth- and eighteenth-century furniture and choice portraits by Nicolas de Larguillère and Louis-Michel Van Loo, as well as a billiard room decorated with battle scenes by Louis

XIV's war painter Jean-Baptiste Martin (known as Martin des Batailles), they are eclipsed by the resplendence of the *Salon Indien* or the "Indian Room."

This Ali Baba's cave of riches is filled with ancient gilded altars, polished bronze Buddhas, bronze temple gongs and votives, as well as a panoply of Indian and Singhalese arms, arranged against a backdrop of richly woven Oriental rugs that cover almost every inch of wall and flooring. It's easy to compare the splendor here with that described in *The Arabian Nights*, when one sees the white marble throne set on a carpeted dais and the solid silver chairs and stools inlaid with mother-of-pearl from India.

The second-floor gallery is mainly devoted to paintings from the Renaissance: full-length portraits from the Italian, French, and Flemish schools and smaller paintings, mostly religious in theme. Off this lengthy gallery are the château's private apartments, including Nélie's lovely celadon green bedroom, furnished with a Louis XV canopy bed made with gilded wood, and containing an exceptional collection of portraits, including works by François Boucher, Jean-Baptiste Greuze, Sir Joshua Reynolds, and Rosalba Carriera.

Most surprising of all are the rooms devoted to Jean-Jacques Rousseau, containing a valuable collection of the philosopher's documents and personal memorabilia that was presented to the Institut de France by the Marquis de Girardin's heirs. (Girardin, a liberal French aristocrat, hosted Rousseau at his estate in Ermenonville during the last months of the philosopher's life.) Seeing the philosopher's musical scores, numerous letters, books, and pamphlets, one cannot help but be impressed and moved by the multi-faceted nature of this eminent thinker.

More than a year after Nélie Jacquemart-André died on May 15, 1912, the Institut de France (to whom she had left Chaalis and her mansion in Paris), was still receiving her final acquisitions—fifty-eight crates from Florence, ten from Venice, as well as paintings and a bust from Milan.

The essence of her dream had been accomplished. In her will, she wrote: "The walls, ruins, château, King's chapel and entire property should be maintained, so that this remains an area of visitation and rest for all French people. Thus will continue one of the most beautiful panoramas, protected from the false civilization that invades, smothers and destroys everything." After a visit to this resplendent sanctuary dedicated to the celebration of art and beauty, one can appreciate how amply—and respectfully—the wishes of Nélie Jacquemart-André have been fulfilled.

THIS LIFE-SIZE CARVED STAG OVER THE FIREPLACE HOOD
WAS MODELED AFTER A LIVE ANIMAL CAUGHT IN THE WOODS NEARBY.

Le Domaine du Château de Monte-Cristo

The Monte-Cristo Estate and Castle

78560 Le Port Marly
Tel: (01) 39–16–49–49

Open to the public
Tuesday through Sunday
10:00 A.M. to 6:00 P.M.,
April 1 through November 1.
Open year-round to groups
with reservations.

Access:
- By train, S.N.C.F.: Gare St-Lazare, direction Marly-le-Roi. Bus C.G.E.A. No. 10, get off at Square de Monte-Cristo, take the Montferrands footpath to the estate.

- By Metro/R.E.R.: Take Line A from Châtelet to Saint-Germain-en-Laye, then take the Bus C.G.E.A. No. 10, get off at Square de Monte-Cristo, take the Montferrands footpath to the estate.

- By car: Take the Nationale 13 from La Défense, direction Saint Germain-en-Laye, until you see the sign for Marly-le-Roi, then take the overpass of the Nationale 13, to the Avenue de l'Europe at Marly-le-Roi, where you will see a sign for "Château de Monte-Cristo." Follow the signage until you reach the estate.

IN 1844, when Alexandre Dumas, author of *The Three Musketeers*, *The Count of Monte-Cristo*, and *The Queen Margot* was at the height of his success, he fell under the spell of a magnificent property, Montferrands at Port-Marly, overlooking the valley of the Seine, between Saint-Germain-en-Laye and the outskirts of Paris. Since money was no object, he bought up enough parcels of land from nine different owners to create an estate of more than four acres—without bothering about a single notarized contract!

Although he originally intended to build a small house in the country, his whimsical imagination caused him to

REFLECTED IN THE MIRROR IS JACQUES-EMILE BLANCHE'S 1889 FULL-LENGTH
PORTRAIT OF JEANINE DUMAS, THE DAUGHTER OF ALEXANDRE DUMAS FILS;
ON THE MANTEL IS THE MARBLE BUST OF
HIS OTHER DAUGHTER, COLETTE, AT AGE FOURTEEN, BY JULES FRANCESCHI.

A VIEW OF THE MONTE-CRISTO CHÂTEAU AND
THE "MOAT" AROUND THE CHÂTEAU D'IF, WHERE DUMAS WOULD
SEEK REFUGE FROM HIS HORDES OF GUESTS.

decide upon a small Renaissance château instead.

"You're going to trace an English park in the midst of which I want a Renaissance château facing a Gothic pavilion surrounded by water," Dumas told his architect, Hippolyte Durand, according to documents

works that flowed from the owner's prolific pen. Whereas the four-sided edifice was partly inspired by the Château d'Anet in the Loire Valley, the profusion of decorative embellishment makes it seem more like a Disney creation than a Renaissance structure.

Over the main entrance is the coat of arms of Davy de la Pailleterie, the ancestors of Dumas. The novelist's father, Thomas Alexandre Dumas, whose portrait hangs in the museum, was the son of the Marquis Davy de la Pailleterie, a wealthy plantation owner in Santo Domingo. His mother was a freed slave who lived on the plantation. Dumas, a born extrovert, never hid the fact that he was of mixed blood, which earned him the nickname *"le Nègre."*

Over the doorway is a stone portrait of Dumas himself, surrounded by a mask and two griffons, and accompanied by this motto: *"J'aime qui m'ayme."* ("I love those who love me.") On the first floor, above every window, one can make out the medallion portraits of the great writers whom the author wished to honor in his personal pantheon: Homer, Virgil, Dante, Shakespeare, Corneille, Lope de Vega, Goethe, Casimir Delavigne, Chateaubriand, and Alphonse de Lamartine.

Even though Dumas's literary reputation has proved to be as lasting as that of the authors he admired, his residency at Monte-Cristo was short-lived. Less than a year after his noteworthy housewarming (there were 600 guests, although only 50 of them had actually been invited), he was forced to sell his estate and flee to Belgium to evade his numerous creditors.

While the interior has undergone important restorations—thanks largely to the Association des Amis d'Alexandre Dumas, who saved the

from the period.—"But, Monsieur Dumas, the ground is made of clay. Your buildings will slide," the architect warned. Undaunted, Dumas ordered: "Monsieur Durand, you will dig until you reach bedrock, and you will make me two floors of cellars and arcades."—"That will cost you a few hundred thousand francs!" exclaimed Durand. Dumas's reply: "I hope so."

Much to everyone's astonishment, the estate envisioned by the wildly fanciful author was built entirely in keeping with his instructions. Although the architect's original estimate was 48,000 francs, the final cost was more than 200,000 francs. (Residents of Port Marly named the estate after Dumas's popular novel.)

The biscuit-colored château that boasts two turrets, was built between 1845 and 1847, and is as fantastic in conception as many of the over 300

mansion from demolition in 1969—visitors should not expect to find it filled with Dumas's personal furnishings. All that remains of the original interior is the *Chambre Mauresque* (the Moorish Chamber), fortunately spared and superbly restored in 1985 thanks to the generosity of the King of Morocco, Hassan II, himself an ardent admirer of the author's work.

This room, on the second floor, is without a doubt the Monte-Cristo's *pièce de résistance*. In October 1846, while the château was being built, Dumas was sent to Algeria at the request of the French government, to gather impressions of the country France had conquered in 1830. During his stay with the Bey of Tunis, the writer became enamored with Moorish art and architecture, and obtained permission from his host to bring back two artists, Hadji Younis and his son Muhammad, who would create the rich and intricate decor that Dumas wanted. (This is one of the few extant examples of a Moorish interior in Europe.)

Sketchy accounts are all that remain of the original arrangement of the château's rooms: on the ground floor, there were two salons, a boudoir, and a dining room; on the second floor—apart from the Moorish Chamber—a parlor and Dumas's bedroom; on the top floor, three guest rooms, as well as a library. (The servants' quarters and stables were on the other side of the house and are now in private hands.)

Although the Association des Amis d'Alexandre Dumas has painstakingly assembled many of the author's private papers, paintings, and other memorabilia pertaining to Dumas and his family—all of which make for a fascinating visit—the only piece of furniture it has been able to buy back is a dark, heavy wooden secretary, now kept in one of the ground-floor salons. In the dining room, one senses the spirit of Dumas, the bon vivant, in his heavy monogrammed silver tableware, dishes, and glasses,

THE MOORISH CHAMBER WAS RESTORED THANKS TO THE GENEROSITY OF HASSAN II, KING OF MOROCCO, AN ADMIRER OF THE WORK OF ALEXANDRE DUMAS.

which take their place alongside his last published work, the *Dictionnaire de la Cuisine*.

It's a pity that nothing else is left of the extravagant decor at Monte-Cristo. Visitors must content themselves with the bill of sale dated Sunday, May 21, 1848, which provides an indication of the fabulous treasures amassed by the profligate writer. According to the bailiff, M. Chaix, the sale included furniture of all kinds, modern as well as antique, Gothic, Medieval, and Renaissance, a piano with six and a half octaves, arms and armor, clocks, statues, paintings, pastels, as well as watercolors by Décamps, Delacroix, Boulanger, Jadin, and Huët, among others. Everything was sold, even the author's wine cellar and horses, who were appropriately christened Athos, Porthos, Aramis, Dantès, and Haydée, all famous characters drawn from his books.

Life at Monte-Cristo could sometimes be as intense and as melodramatic as the writer's works.

THIS MARBLE BUST OF HENRIETTE DUMAS, THE SECOND WIFE
OF ALEXANDRE DUMAS FILS, WAS SCULPTED BY JULES FRANCESCHI.

THIS STONE PORTRAIT OF ALEXANDRE DUMAS ORNAMENTS THE ENTRANCE OF HIS CHÂTEAU.

A known womanizer, Dumas was always in the company of one mistress or another, most of whom were either actresses or courtesans.

Still, there were plenty of other distractions, including celebrated séances with mediums and hypnotists. Every Sunday, Dumas would host a dinner for twenty, which he often liked to help prepare himself—although he was better known as a raconteur than as a chef.

In addition to playing host to an endless round of guests and hangers-on, the writer kept an extensive if not unusual menagerie, which at one time included fourteen dogs, among them his favorite pointer Pritchard, Mouton the terrier, Tombo, the "fake-terrier," a King Charles of doubtful pedigree, and Turco, a hairless Turkish dog, as well as three monkeys, a golden pheasant, a rooster named César, and a cat named Mysouff II.

When this intense whirl of uninvited guests, gossip, and entertaining began to overwhelm the writer, he would flee to his charming Château d'If. This tiny, two-story Gothic pavilion nestled on top of a hill (with a single room on each floor) is surrounded by a moat filled with water and is accessible only via a drawbridge. Its quaint façade is ornamented with white stones engraved with the titles of seventy-eight of the author's works. When Dumas worked here, the downstairs room had an azure ceiling strewn with golden stars and a Gothic-style fireplace decorated with coats of arms and blue hangings. Dressed in pants of white ticking and a comfortable shirt, the writer would sit at his swivel chair and write on an old convent refectory table.

While Dumas's writing at Monte-Cristo was limited (it's easy to see why), his unbounded creativity was fully expressed in the charmingly wild gardens surrounding his château. With its grottos, rock gardens, waterfalls, brooks, rose bushes, and verdant knolls, it's the kind of setting that captivates visitors of all ages.

Should Dumas return to his beloved Monte-Cristo today, he would see there is no trace left of the calm provincialism that characterized Port Marly when he lived there. Still, he would be delighted to discover that his estate has remained an oasis of serenity and peacefulness. Perhaps he would also chuckle at the thought that the property which led to his financial ruin has now attained the status of a national monument—a distinction befitting one of the world's most celebrated authors of adventurous and high-spirited historical novels.

La Maison de Balzac

The House of Balzac

47, Rue Raynouard
75016 Paris
Tel: (01) 42–24–56–38

Open Tuesday through Sunday
10:00 A.M. to 5:40 P.M.

Metro: Passy, La Muette
Bus: 32, 52, 72

"I AM WRITING at eight o'clock in the morning, with the sun filtering through my window, wreathing my desk, drapes and papers in a red scarf. Surely there are enough omens here. Are they to be trusted? The beauty of this early morning is difficult to conceive. The sky is blue, with a few clouds accentuating its intensity, and the heights of Issy and Meudon are bathed in light; I can see them as I write. No! this must surely be God's way of forecasting happiness!"

Balzac wrote these lines to his beloved Russian countess, Eveline de Hanska, on January 1, 1844, from

THIS OVERHEAD VIEW OF BALZAC'S HOUSE AND GARDEN SUGGESTS A PEACEFUL REFUGE. AMONG THE AUTHOR'S RARE GUESTS WAS THE ROMANTIC POET GERARD DE NERVAL.

BY LEAVING HIS HOME FROM THE RUE BERTON (FORMERLY THE RUE DU ROC), BALZAC COULD EASILY REACH THE CAPITAL. OTHER THAN THE NAME, MUCH OF THE RUE BERTON HAS REMAINED VIRTUALLY UNCHANGED SINCE THE AUTHOR LIVED HERE.

the study in his modest lodgings in Passy, which became part of Paris in 1860.

His words were to prove prophetic. In flight from his creditors after a disastrous investment in a pineapple plantation at his country estate, Les Jardies at Sèvres, Balzac had retreated to this apartment on the Rue Basse (today Rue Raynouard), where he lived and wrote from October 1840 until April 1847. It was in this house, first built in the eighteenth century, and today known as *La Maison de Balzac* (The House of Balzac), that he was to correct the whole of *The Human Comedy* and write some of his greatest works: *A Dark Affair, La Rabouilleuse, Cousin Bette, Cousin Pons,* and *Splendors and Miseries of Courtesans.*

This residence not only became a place of feverish productivity, but a convenient refuge with easy access to the capital. Leaving his home from the Rue du Roc entrance (now the Rue Berton), Balzac could easily reach the Route de Versailles (now Avenue de New York) and board a ferry to the center of Paris.

Those few visitors who came to see the writer had to pass first through a house on the Rue Basse (which no longer exists), then proceed down some steps, and only after crossing a small courtyard were able to reach the writer's retreat.

Although the area has changed substantially, visitors to the House of Balzac can still enjoy a delightful respite from the smog of Paris in the museum's verdant garden overlooking the city, where the writer used to pick the first lilacs and roses of the season.

Living there under the pseudonym of Monsieur de Breugnol, inspired by his housekeeper Louise Breugniot (who appears in the novels as Madame de Breugnol or Brugnol), Balzac occupied six rooms: a dining

IT WAS IN THIS GARDEN, STILL FILLED WITH THE ROSES AND LILACS BALZAC LOVED, THAT THE AUTHOR OF *THE HUMAN COMEDY* WOULD WALK AND DREAM. THE EIFFEL TOWER, SEEN HERE IN THE DISTANCE, WOULD BE BUILT IN 1889, ALMOST FORTY YEARS AFTER HIS DEATH.

room, bedroom, sitting room, study, guest room, and kitchen. In 1910, the eighteenth-century house was saved from demolition and turned into a private museum. The City of Paris took it over in 1949, a year before the centenary of Balzac's death.

Today the restored building includes Balzac's garden apartment, as well as the rooms and outhouses originally occupied by the other tenants, and spans three levels between the Rue Raynouard and the Rue Berton. The ground floor facing the Rue Berton (formerly stables and other lodgings), now contains a handsome library of over 10,000 books and manuscripts available to scholars who come from all over the world to consult them.

Only the study is preserved virtually as it was in Balzac's day, with its garnet-red-flocked velvet walls, colored glass windows, wooden work table, and high-backed tapestry-covered chair. It's easy to envision the writer dressed in his monk's habit, "harnessed," as he put it, to this small table, which—as he wrote to Madame Hanska—has "witnessed all my miseries, known all my enterprises, heard all my thoughts, so much so that my arm has worn it down from writing."

Among the few other personal objects in the study are Balzac's red and white porcelain coffeepot with his initials, recalling his excessive use of this stimulant, which he endowed with great powers of inspiration. Also in the study are two marble sculptures of Balzac made during his lifetime: the first by Alessandro Puttinati showing the writer in his famous monk's robe; the second, a massive head by David d'Angers.

According to Balzac's letters the study's walls were once covered with pictures, but only two remain today: a portrait of Madame Hanska and an engraving of Wierzschownia Castle, her lakeside estate in the Ukraine.

Facing his writing table is a wooden Christ inside an elaborate frame that Balzac attributed to Edmé Bouchardon. Eager to impress the wealthy Madame Hanska, whom he was then courting, Balzac wrote: "I have, dear angel, a sculpted masterpiece of Christ! A Christ in wood by Bouchardon estimated at 3,000 francs, and which Madame de Brugnol was able to buy, by accident, for 150 francs!" The novelist, an inveterate collector of antiques and bibelots, tended to exaggerate the value of his "finds" and was often misled. (The actual provenance of the Christ has never been definitively established.)

The real masterpieces, of course, were Balzac's novels with their over 3,000 characters, whose extensive genealogy is now on display in the museum's basement. It was while he lived in the Rue Basse that Balzac drew up an agreement with his publishers, Furne, Hetzel, Paulin, and Dubochet, that granted them exclusive rights to print and sell his complete works under the collective title *The Human Comedy*.

Those visitors wishing to learn more about the writer's family and entourage won't be disappointed. The House of Balzac contains period portraits of both his parents, as well as his eldest sister, Laure, to whom he dedicated *A Start in Life*. The novelist's father, Bernard-François

BALZAC'S DESK, CHAIR, BOOKS, AND MONOGRAMMED COFFEEPOT IN HIS STUDY. THE MASSIVE MARBLE BUST BY DAVID D'ANGERS WAS REFUSED BY THE SALON, BECAUSE ITS DEDICATION *"TO HIS FRIEND DE BALZAC. P.J. DAVID D'ANGERS. 1844"* WAS IN VIOLATION OF THE JURY'S RULES.

Balzac, a passionate advocate of liberty and a disciple of the Encyclopedists, prospered both before and after the French Revolution. Working his way up the municipal ladder, he eventually became deputy mayor of Tours. Then, in 1814, he moved to Paris with his family, where he managed to retire with a sizeable pension. He died on June 19, 1829, the same year his son published *The Chouans*, the first novel written under his own name.

Rather late in life, when he was fifty-one, Bernard-François Balzac had married nineteen-year-old Laure Sallembier, Balzac's mother, who came from a family of rich drapers in Paris. As her portrait reveals, she was a rather pretty and cultured coquette. Balzac felt deprived of her affection as a child, however, and this was something he held against her for much of his life. Yet, despite their stormy relationship, Madame Balzac lived for a while at the Rue Basse.

The museum allocates an entire room to the portraits and mementos of the woman who was to play the most central role in his life— Madame Eveline de Hanska, born in 1805 into a family of Polish nobility. A delicate ivory miniature painted at the time of her marriage to Count Hanski reveals a sensitive, cultivated woman with dark curly hair and eyes to match. Fluent in French and German, Madame Hanska first encountered Balzac through his books. Between 1832 and 1848, the novelist kept up a voluminous correspondence with the woman he was to call "The Foreigner."

Balzac first met Madame Hanska in September 1833 in Neuchâtel, Switzerland, when she was on holiday there with her husband. Although he saw her again the following year in Geneva, and the year after in Vienna, there was a gap of eight years before they met again in Saint Petersburg. When Count Hanski died in 1841, Balzac hoped to marry his beloved countess at long last, but she, hesitating, continued to postpone any wedding plans.

Eager to assure his cherished mistress that she would continue to live in the style to which she was accustomed, the novelist purchased an apartment in the Rue Fortunée (now the Rue Balzac) in September 1846. He himself devised the interior decoration down to the most minute detail, spending thousands of francs on antiques and bric-à-brac. All that remains of this splendor is a magnificent inlaid door to a sitting room, and a bookcase.

Although Balzac spent the last two years of his life on Madame Hanska's estate in Wierzschownia, it was only on March 14, 1850, that the couple married in Berdichev. Five months later, on August 18, Balzac died at his palatial home in the Rue Fortunée, without the comfort of his bride's presence. The major portion of the writer's manuscripts and correspondence was purchased by an erudite Belgian collector, Viscount Spoelberch de Lovenjoul, who donated them to the Institut de France.

While the House of Balzac contains fascinating memorabilia pertaining to the writer and his entourage, the museum aims to be much more than hallowed ground honoring one of the world's great novelists. According to curator Judith Meyer-Petit, its collections are continuously growing, and temporary exhibits relating to the author's work and epoch are held throughout the year. "These exhibitions attest to the modernity of *The Human Comedy*," she says. "The House of Balzac is in constant development, a living organism, just like *The Human Comedy*."

Le Musée des Arts d'Afrique et d'Océanie

The Museum of African and Oceanic Arts

293, Avenue Daumesnil
75012 Paris
Tel: (01) 44-74-84-80

Open Monday through Friday
from 10:00 A.M. to Noon and
1:30 P.M. to 5:20 P.M.;
Saturday and Sunday from
12:30 P.M. to 5:50 P.M. (Only the
Aquarium is open from
10:00 A.M. to 5:50 P.M.).
Closed Tuesday.

Metro: Porte Dorée
Bus: 46, P.C.

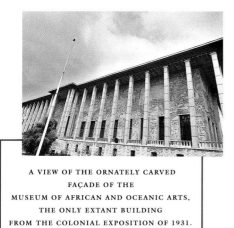

A VIEW OF THE ORNATELY CARVED
FAÇADE OF THE
MUSEUM OF AFRICAN AND OCEANIC ARTS,
THE ONLY EXTANT BUILDING
FROM THE COLONIAL EXPOSITION OF 1931.

I F Y O U W O U L D like to see
live crocodiles, antique diamond
brooches and tiaras, as well as an
exceptional collection of African and
Oceanic art under a single roof, the
place to visit is the highly unusual
Museum of African and Oceanic Arts,
a stone's throw from the Bois de
Vincennes and its zoological park.

This three-story museum (which
boasts a tropical aquarium in the
basement) was built by the renowned
architects Léon Jausseley and Albert
Leprade for the 1931 Colonial
Exposition. Its edifice is a remarkable
fusion of 1930s Neoclassical
architecture and exoticism, intended
when it was inaugurated to pay
homage to the economic and political
ties of France to her once numerous
colonies. Nowhere is this more
evident than in the cement bas-relief
decorating its lengthy colonnaded
façade—"a stone tapestry" sculpted
by Alfred Janniot (1889–1969), who
also decorated the famed *Ile de France*
cruise ship.

Like many public buildings in
Paris, this palatial museum (classified
as a historic monument in 1987
because of its unique façade, roofing,
entrance gates, and 1930s ground-
floor interiors) has changed its name
and mission several times. When it
first opened in 1931, it was known as
the *Musée des Colonies* (The Colonial
Museum); in 1935, it was renamed
the *Musée de la France d'Outre-Mer*
(The Museum of Overseas France)
and was appended to the Colonial
Ministry. In 1960, through the
initiative of André Malraux, then
France's Minister of Culture (as well
as a connoisseur of African art), the

THESE STUNNING TOTEMS WERE CREATED BY ABORIGINES
LIVING ON THE BATHURST AND MELVILLE ISLANDS
OFF THE NORTHERN COAST OF AUSTRALIA.

museum was given a new mandate, as well as a new name: the Museum of African and Oceanic Arts.

Malraux's reorganization turned out to be more far-reaching than a mere name change. The museum was placed under the aegis of the Ministry of Culture, and allocated a budget that allowed it to double the size of its original holdings. Moreover, it was given an aesthetic orientation encompassing two continents—Africa and Oceania—and three cultural regions, the Maghreb (North Africa), the civilizations from the sub-Saharan region, and the archipelagoes of the South Pacific. At the same time, the Tropical Aquarium, which had been specifically created for the Colonial Exposition, was completely refurbished.

In the aquarium's semi-darkness the visitor is confronted by an extraordinary array of flora and fauna from all over the world, including so-called "living fossil" fish from Africa, whose ancestors originated 300 million years ago, two-meter-long white sharks from the Indo-Pacific Ocean, vivid psychedelic-patterned Mandarin fish, and breathtakingly graceful, but deadly Scorpion fish, whose feathery wings hide venomous barbs. Still, for many, the aquarium's chief attraction is the immense pit containing three mesmerizing crocodiles that actually are supposed to date back to the Colonial Exposition!

In a concerted effort to bridge a colonial past and France's current geopolitical situation, this atypical museum has carefully preserved the 1930s colonialistic decor for its intrinsic aesthetic value. The 600-square-meter fresco in the *Salle des Fêtes,* by Pierre Ducos de la Haille (1889–1972) and his students—intended to show how the French virtues of Peace, Justice, Work, Art, Industry, and Freedom have benefited the four corners of the globe—retains its value as an historical document, even if France's various contributions in this dimension might be assessed somewhat differently today.

Aficionados of Art Deco will appreciate the museum's two magnificent public rooms, built to welcome important guests to the Colonial Exposition. The *Salon d'Afrique* in particular, with its frescoes by Louis Bouquet (1885–1925), and its magnificent ebony desk inlaid with ivory and sharkskin, as well as its famous leather "elephant" armchairs by Jacques-Emile Ruhlmann, represents a high point in the period's decorative arts.

The museum's outstanding collections from the Pacific region are displayed in two rooms on the

SHOWN HERE IS ONE OF THE THREE CROCODILES LEFT IN THE MUSEUM'S AQUARIUM SINCE THE COLONIAL EXPOSITION OF 1931, WHICH CONTINUE TO ENTHRALL VISITORS OF ALL AGES.

ground floor. The exhibition space allocated to Australian art not only presents a handsome group of carved and decorated funerary poles made by the Tiwi tribe from the north of Australia, but also a precious collection of bark paintings crafted by the Aborigines from Arnhem Land on the North Coast. These strikingly abstract works, made with different shades of ground earth, are presumed to be simple reproductions of clannish symbols used in body painting, preparatory sketches for rock paintings, as well as aide-mémoires for the recitation of ancient myths. "We have close to 300 of these bark paintings in our collections, more than any other museum in Europe or the United States," notes Dominique Taffin, the Oceanic arts curator. "Because they are so fragile, we can only exhibit a few at a time."

THIS RIVETING MBEMBÉ SEATED WOODEN STATUE FROM EASTERN NIGERIA, IS A FRAGMENT OF A SACRIFICIAL DRUM.

The museum also prides itself on being the only institution in France to possess a series of contemporary paintings (early 1990s) by Aborigines from Alice Springs in the continent's Central Desert. Notable for their geometrical forms consisting of lines, circles, arcs, ovals, and zig-zags, these works represent myths that go back to the dawn of time, which have been transmitted from father to son over the past 20,000 to 30,000 years. These collaborative and ritualistic works, produced by several artists, pay homage to the dingo, the emu, the crocodile, and the sacred python—ancestral mythical beings who, according to the Aborigines, continue to intervene in the world of the living.

Compared with Australia, Melanesian art is notable for its great diversity of forms and materials. The museum's collection includes funerary art from the Bismarck Archipelago, arrows and a rough model of a chieftain's hut from New Caledonia, and

THIS REMARKABLE WOODEN ELEPHANT MASK IS ONE OF THE FIFTY-THREE PIECES FROM THE CAMEROON GRASSLANDS, DONATED BY PIERRE HARTER.

THIS GOLD-THREAD CAPE AND
SILK CAFTAN AND THE BRASS BRAZIER
SUPPORTING A TEA KETTLE WERE ONCE USED
BY A WEALTHY NORTH AFRICAN BRIDE.

THIS RARE BIRD-SHAPED PENDANT FROM MOROCCO
WAS MADE BY CRAFTSMEN IN THE SEVENTEENTH CENTURY.

wonderful mixed-media Melanesian ritual dance masks, half-human, half-beast, made of wood, dried earth, basketry, and cloth, and decorated with fibers, feathers, shells, leaves, and paints made from ground earth, shells, and even charcoal.

The museum's extensive African collections are divided into two parts: on the ground floor and the second floor can be found the art of Central and West Africa; while on the third and top floors the visitor will encounter the collections from North Africa, notably Morocco, Algeria, and Tunisia.

The art of West Africa is represented by highly stylized and geometric works from the Sudanese grasslands, such as masks and statuettes by the Dogon and the Bambara tribes of Mali, as well as by the more naturalistic statuary from the Baoulé and Anyi tribes of the Ivory Coast. One of the most outstanding masks is a nineteenth-century Gouro Bété funerary mask from the Ivory Coast, once owned by Dadaist Tristan Tzara: made of dark polished wood and monkey hair, its anguished and poignant expression denotes great artistry as well as sensitivity.

Among the objects from Central Africa, it is essential to mention the one-of-a-kind colorful royal patchwork tapestries from the Fon kings of Benin (now southern Nigeria), finely carved ivory statuettes and elephant tusks from the Congo, as well as remarkable wooden sculptures by the Yoruba (Nigeria), Ibo (Nigeria), Bamileke (Cameroon), Fang (Gabon), and Luba (Zaire) tribes.

Still, by far the most important and choice grouping of Central African art at the museum is a group of fifty-three statues, ritual masks, and sculpted posts from chieftains' huts, gathered together in a permanent exhibit entitled, "The Sculptor Kings: Art and Power in the Grasslands of the Cameroon." The collection, dramatically presented in a dimly lit gallery that enhances the power and mystery of each work, was left to the museum in 1991 by Pierre Harter, a doctor who had been practicing in the mountains of Western Cameroon since 1957 and who, over time, became one of the leading experts in the area's art and culture. Not only do these artists from the mountainous grasslands of the Cameroon reveal unusual variety and artistry (twenty of the fifty-three works are considered to be masterpieces), but thanks to Harter's scrupulous scholarship, the origins and significance of each piece are documented for the visitor's benefit.

The museum's North African collection is notable for its exhibits of jewelry, embroidered and woven textiles, Berber rugs and lusterware. "We have an exceptional collection of woven Moroccan rugs made by the Berbers and embroideries from Morocco, Tunisia, and Algeria," notes Marie-France Vivier, curator of North African arts.

Still, among the most impressive pieces on display are exquisite pieces of jewelry, including a remarkable diamond and white gold tiara and brooch, made during the Ottoman Empire by an Italian jeweler named Sanghinetti.

The Museum of African and Oceanic Arts both delights and dazzles with its rich and fascinating range of objects—be they animate or inanimate. Viewing them not only engenders both awe and admiration for these distant lands and their peoples, but also expands one's artistic and cultural horizon to include the wondrous variety of African and Oceanic art.

THESE VERTICAL SLIT DRUMS WERE MADE BY THE VANUATU TRIBE IN THE NEW HEBRIDES.

Le Musée des Arts Forains

The Museum of Carnival Art

Les Pavillons de Bercy
53, Avenue des Terroirs de France
75012 Paris
Tel: (01) 43–40–16–22

Group and individual visits on
Saturday and Sunday by
prior appointment.

Metro: Bercy, Dugommier
Bus: 24, 62

Every Saturday and Sunday afternoon in the restored former wine depots at Bercy (at one time renowned for being the last locale where duty-free alcohol was available in Paris), the curtain goes up on one of the most original and fantastic of spectacles: an old-fashioned carnival featuring antique merry-go-rounds, swings, shooting galleries, games of chance—even a live puppet theater.

Suddenly, three of the merry-go-rounds are set in motion, their glowing horses, cows, donkeys, pigs, and swans moving to the words and melody of a hauntingly sentimental popular song. Overhead, horses separated from their carousel gallop through the air like a group of flying Pegasuses. A dazzling Baroque

IN THE FOREGROUND IS THE FIRST CHILDREN'S MERRY-GO-ROUND
WITH "JUMPING FIGURES," BUILT AROUND 1900;
IN THE BACKGROUND, A CAROUSEL OF MOTORCYCLES AND
AUTOMOBILES, MADE IN LILLE AROUND 1925.

Venetian gondola with its original paint, lavishly decorated with copper inlay, convex Bohemian mirrors and painted landscapes, and upholstered in plush red velvet, invites visitors to embark on the kind of journey that only dreams are made of. And then there is the towering, bare-breasted, Phrygian-capped *Marianne* made of painted wood, brandishing the *tricolore* and inviting the assembled crowd to join in the frolic.

Welcome to the Museum of Carnival Art in the Pavillons de Bercy, consisting of six handsome brick buildings located along two tree-lined cobblestone streets, a stone's throw from the Seine and the awesomely vast glass and steel building housing the Ministry of Finance. Filled with twleve merry-go-rounds, thirty amusement park stalls and attractions, and over 1,500 collector's items, it is the only museum in France devoted exclusively to the art of these popular attractions.

This fantastic museum is the creation of Jean-Paul Favand, whose passion for theater and antiques led him to become an early collector of this once neglected art.

"Twenty-five years ago these objects were completely scorned," he recalls. "France is a country so rich in objects that for a long time, no one bothered with those you see here. Moreover, because so much of carnival art was in a deplorable state, virtually broken into pieces, it was hard for people to appreciate its intrinsic beauty."

The collector's bug took Favand over when he discovered that some discarded fragments of carved wooden wainscoting, were in fact, the remains of a carousel "salon"—the

IT WASN'T LONG AFTER THE CREATION OF MICKEY MOUSE
THAT CARTOON CHARACTERS MADE THEIR APPEARANCE AT THE FAIRGROUND--
HERE IS MICKEY WITH THE EARS OF MORTIMER,
TWO DIFFERENT VERSIONS OF GOOFY, A PIPE-SMOKING DONALD DUCK,
A DWARF, AND A FAUN. (© THE WALT DISNEY COMPANY.)

most fabulous of the amusement park attractions around 1900—once containing an enormous merry-go-round, a large bar, a ballroom, as well as penny arcades and games of chance. "I have old photographs showing that these carousel salons were so enormous that, when shipped, they took up as many as thirty rail cars," notes Favand.

As is true of so many collections embarked upon haphazardly in the heat of collector's fever, this one attained such amplitude that, eventually, Favand was forced to move it from a warehouse on the Rue de Provence to a vast 4,000-square-meter shed in Gentilly, until it finally found its present home in Paris. This turned out to be the requisite space needed for repairing and restoring what had become a motley agglomeration of fairground carousels, scenery, sculptures, and decors that had once enchanted generations of families across Europe.

An invaluable compilation of period archives (including catalogues listing manufacturers of carnival art) enabled Favand to authenticate his acquisitions and to return them, when feasible, to their original state. Consultations with a number of European fairground operators assisted in creating the museum's enchanting ambiance which unites the architecture, paintings, sculptures, and lighting of popular, old-fashioned amusement parks.

Carnival art emerged during the second half of the nineteenth century, in tandem with the Industrial Revolution and the widespread rural migration to the cities. During this era of mechanization and factories, of offices and sweatshops, there arose a demand among the new class of urban workers for escapist entertainment that was both spectacular and affordable. A number of shrewd and enterprising showmen—including the movie producers Pathé and Gaumont—were to profit handsomely from devising amusements whose artful illusionism enabled the working poor and lower middle classes to momentarily put aside their daily burdens.

At the height of the amusement park era, different schools of carnival artists were working in enterprises throughout Europe, notably in Germany, Belgium, England, and France. Although most of these artists remain unknown, some names have endured: Coquereau and Maréchal and Gustave Bayol from Angers, Frederich Heyn from Neustadt, Alexander Devos from Ghent, and Johann Radschek from Vienna— all of whose works are represented in Favand's collection.

Carnival art took its inspiration from a multitude of popular rituals and traditions, including the medieval country fair, rural feast-days, and princely spectacles, as well as from myths, legends, and folklore. Later, amusement parks would integrate the latest modern inventions into their rides and attractions, including automobiles, bicycles, planes, and motorcycles—examples of which are displayed in this museum.

The carousels' magnificent galloping steeds are a throwback to the days of knights and jousting tournaments, while their columns, garlands, trellises, and their paintings of voluptuous nymphs and cherubim are a distant reminder of the edenic pleasures of Boucher, Fragonard, and Watteau.

Although the amusement park bestiary is dominated by the horse,

THIS ELEGANTLY RAFFISH
RED-VELVET MECHANICAL SHOOTING GALLERY
FROM LILLE, C.1900, FEATURES
A SERIES OF BRILLIANT POLYCHROME TARGETS
COMPOSED OF TINWARE,
MADE IN AUSTRIA AROUND 1900
BY THE VIENNESE ARTIST, JOHANN RADSCHEK.

THESE 1896 PATHÉ FILM PROJECTORS ONCE BELONGED TO THE GAUMONT FAMILY.
BOTH CHARLES PATHÉ AND LÉON GAUMONT WERE FAIRGROUND OPERATORS
BEFORE GOING INTO THE MOVIE BUSINESS.

the museum's carousels show that by the end of the nineteenth century, such plebeian farm animals as cows, pigs, donkeys, rabbits, and goats had been added to the merry-go-round, perhaps out of a sense of nostalgia for a vanishing rural heritage. The glories of French and German colonies are also evoked by the appearance of wild animals, including elephants, giraffes, and zebras. Later, with the widespread popularity of cartoon characters, some enterprising amusement park operators devised their own versions of Mickey Mouse, Donald Duck, and Popeye, examples of which are also in the museum.

The garish and tantalizing decor of the city's theaters and music-halls also was a source of inspiration, as is evident in a splendidly restored theatrical shooting gallery, decorated with mirrors, red velvet, gold fringes, and gaudy beadwork.

"Carnival art is a decorative art that was designed to appeal to the greatest number of people," explains Favand. "The concept was to give a notion of luxury and the exotic to people who didn't customarily have it in their lives."

It would be hard to find an art form with a greater fusion of artistic periods—Rococo, Baroque, Art Nouveau, Art Deco, to name but a few—all of them executed with captivating bravura. "This type of decorative art was a pastiche of the fine arts, and its creators had no fear of borrowing from different periods and styles," Favand notes.

Every imaginable decorative technique was used by the makers of carousels, from gilding, silvering, mirroring, and lace-making to tapestry-making, and brasswork. Distorting mirrors, trompe-l'oeil, false perspectives, and reverses in scale were all part of the dramatic and hypnotic effects freely used by carnival artists. These illusory and fantastic decors would later exert a visible influence upon advertising and the cinema, as well as upon theme parks such as Disneyland and Walt Disney World.

At the same time, carnival art with its sensational colors and distorted figures had a significant influence on twentieth-century art forms, and has often been linked to Expressionism, Hyperrealism, as well as to Naïve and Primitive art.

While most amusement park attractions were conceived for the purpose of diversion, some of them were also educational. In addition to the usual freaks and sideshows, there were demonstrations of chemistry, electricity, and magnetism, as well as of the first motion pictures. The Pathé family's first movie projectors—which were once used to show early motion pictures at the Pathé fairgrounds in Brittany—are among the rarities on display here.

Although the museum's ambiance emphasizes the enchantment and romance of carnival art, it also offers visitors a chance to discover the diversity of mechanical music, particularly popular during the Belle Epoque. Activated by means of rolls, strips, cylinders, disks, or levers set in motion, these mechanical instruments took the place of live musicians and made up for any lack of musical talent. (Even such renowned composers as Handel, Mozart, and Beethoven were commissioned to write pieces for rare mechanical organs.) The museum's extensive collection of these fascinating instruments, now located in the *Salons de Musique,* includes examples of the pianola and the hand-cranked barrel organ, as well as the elaborate cinema organ (once used to accompany silent films), and the orchestrion (a forerunner of the jukebox). Listening to the highly evocative melodies that these instruments are still able to produce, ranging from popular songs to operatic medleys, and seeing them in the midst of an assembly of lifelike wax figures created in the ateliers of the famed Musée Grévin, depicting such famous personalities as the actress Sarah Bernhardt, the novelist Victor Hugo, the painters Auguste Renoir and Henri de Toulouse-Lautrec, as well as the musicians Claude Debussy and Camille Saint-Saens, the visitor feels magically transported to another era.

In an atmosphere that blends the real and the surreal, the alluring and the macabre, the Museum of Carnival Art seems far removed from the familiar streets of Paris and the routine of urban life.

"This museum is the equivalent of an amusement park that makes it possible for people to travel through time, while remaining in one place," notes Favand. "My hope is that people will come here to learn and to dream."

THIS DENTAL CHAIR, COMPLETE WITH A FOOT-OPERATED DENTAL DRILL, WAS A COMMON SIGHT AT FAIRGROUNDS AROUND 1900.

Le Musée des Arts et Traditions Populaires
The Museum of Popular Arts and Traditions

6, Avenue du Mahatma-Gandhi
75016 Paris
Tel: (01) 44–17–60–00

Open every day except Tuesday
9:45 A.M. to 5:15 P.M.

Metro: Sablons
Bus: 73, 82, P.C.

WHEN THE MUSEUM OF
POPULAR ARTS AND TRADITIONS
WAS BUILT IN 1969,
IT WAS ACCLAIMED FOR ITS
INNOVATIVE
ARCHITECTURAL DESIGN.

ADJACENT TO the small zoo and amusement park in the Bois de Boulogne is a strikingly modern edifice consisting of two opposing and sharply intersecting parallelepipeds, built in 1969 by Michel Jausserand and Jean Dubuisson, admirers of Walter Gropius and Mies van der Rohe. It may come as a surprise to learn that behind this epitome of French modern architecture is sheltered a museum that richly illustrates the occupations, customs, and traditions of rural and urban French society dating back to the Gallo-Roman era.

Known as the Museum of Popular Arts and Traditions, it is the brainchild of French ethnographer Georges-Henri Rivière, who—with the encouragement of the Socialist government of Léon Blum—created this museum. (The original museum was located in the Palais de Chaillot at the Trocadéro.)

A man ahead of his time, Rivière assigned research teams during and after World War II to scour the French countryside for objects, documents, and photographs, as well as to record testimonials from local inhabitants. (Many people are unaware that this assignment saved a number of Jewish researchers from being deported to concentration camps.)

The current museum is divided into two parts: the basement (open since 1972) contains a study gallery of vitrines displaying an extensive collection of tools and objects pertaining to many aspects of rural life; the ground floor, or cultural gallery (open since 1975), houses an

THE KITCHEN OF A DAIRY FARM
IN THE HAUTE SAVOIE
SHOWS THE SIMPLE LIFE LED BY MUCH
OF THE FRENCH PEASANTRY
AS LATE AS THE 1950S.

THIS WAS THE TYPICAL COSTUME WORN BY A SHEPHERD
ON THE HEATH AROUND 1880—
THE STILTS PROTECTED HIS FEET FROM MUD AND SNOW
AND ALSO ENABLED HIM TO SURVEY HIS FLOCK.

impressive arrangement of reconstructed rural techniques, occupations, and traditions. While the study gallery is reserved mainly for researchers and ethnologists, the cultural gallery's displays are intended for a general public of all ages.

The black walls and ceilings and the white marble floors of the cultural gallery impart a theatrical quality to the exhibits. "The dim lighting and theatrical effects were quite fashionable at one time," explains Anne-Marie Kefi, the museum's director of press relations. "Even though all the objects are authentic, Rivière wanted the visitor to make the distinction that they were in a museum, which is different from the real world."

The displays in the cultural gallery reveal that, until very recently, many of the tools, occupations, and activities long associated with France, such as the making of bread, wine, and cheese, remained virtually unchanged over the centuries. The words "Gallic tradition" take on an even greater significance when one sees that a sickle for cutting wheat, a plane for planing wood, and a pair of shears for shearing sheep's wool—all tools used early in this century—differ hardly at all from those used during the Gallo-Roman era. The wearing of wooden shoes and the use of wine barrels are as old as Gaul itself, and French tastes in food and drink are just as enduring. For instance, a text by the Roman author Strabon praises Gallic *charcuterie* (pork products). Although it was under Roman domination that the nation's vineyards first took on their now celebrated importance, viniculture was already being practiced prior to Caesar's invasion of Gaul.

France's strong ties to the ancient world are underscored through the museum's whimsical display of a package of *Gauloises bleu* cigarettes and of an original drawing of a popular comic strip hero, *Astérix Le Gaulois*, created after World War II.

At the same time, the museum also documents the impact of industrialization. For instance, whereas a map of 1850 France indicates that almost every region of the country possessed important vineyards, a 1974 map shows that the onslaught of modern roads and rail transportation had shrunk viniculture by more than a third.

Although the exhibits do not dwell upon the cycle of poverty, taxation, and revolt that has marked the history of the French working class, they do illustrate the hardship and privation that have troubled so many of the nation's peasants and artisans. Despite France's important culinary tradition, until after World War II the average Frenchman lived on a grain-based diet, in the form of gruel, bread, or crepes. Meat, fresh fruits, and vegetables rarely made an appearance on the rural table (one exception being salted pork). Until the 1880s, the French peasant rarely drank wine; the most common beverages were water laced with vinegar or fruit-based alcohol. Only on feast days did the rural classes dine on dishes of poultry, game, and other meat, as well as wine and sweet cakes.

A comprehensive step-by-step presentation of wheat and bread production prior to mechanization demonstrates that the methods of soil preparation, planting, and harvesting remained essentially unchanged for almost two thousand years. The French farmer was so faithful to tradition that it was not until the nineteenth century that he replaced his sickle with a scythe, and his flail with a threshing roll. Similarly, as late as 1931, there were still almost 10,500 windmills and watermills compared with 5,482 industrial flour mills. As recently as 1963, these windmills, which once ground up to one hundred kilos of grain a day, were crushing chestnuts for pig feed.

Visitors will be surprised to discover that the Museum of Popular Arts and Traditions was one of the first institutions to use interactive displays. By the mere touch of a button, a vitrine lights up to reveal the *Marianne-toute-seule*, an authentic sail-powered fishing boat built until 1945 at Berck, a port town near Calais. The fishermen's universe comes alive through the swaying boat, the recorded sounds of wailing seagulls, and a narrative describing each facet of the boat and its activities.

Sounds of chopping, cutting, planing, and wood turning animate the reconstructed workshop of Désiré Louvel, the last wood turner to close his shop in 1953 in La Bauge, a small town in Normandy. A taped interview with one of Louvel's former workers, speaking in the local patois, describes each of the manifold steps required to produce a hundred wooden spoons during the course of a twelve-hour day, a job that paid five francs a day in the 1930s.

The sounds of mooing cows, tinkling cattle bells, shepherds' calls, and milk being poured into wooden pails, as well as the various steps of cheese production, bring the visitor into the lives of dairy producers in the Aubrac, a mountainous plain in the Auvergne. The reconstructed wooden shepherd's hut with its straw-laden bed and wooden cheese vats was shared in 1910 by five men working in shifts, and was used for sleeping and eating as well as for making Cantal cheese.

The museum vividly documents the slow changes in rural life through the reconstructed dwelling of a

THIS LOOM FROM THE HAUTE-PYRÉNÉES AT CAMPAN WAS USED AS LATE AS 1961.

Breton couple, Guillaume and
Catherine Deuffic. In this single
room, the family worked, took its
meals, entertained, slept, and
witnessed the progress of the technology that was gradually introduced
into the home. In 1906, the oil lamp
replaced the candle; in 1910, the
ground was covered with cement; in
1930, a stove was added to the fireplace, at the same time that a water
pump was added on to the house.
Finally, in 1941, the house was
electrified, and in 1951, piped with
running water.

Although the Museum of Popular
Arts and Traditions is mainly devoted
to rural occupations and craftsmanship, a portion of the museum has
been set aside to illustrate the changes
in popular entertainment, including
circuses, puppet theaters, festivals, and
parades. Vitrines devoted to richly
ornamented regional costumes,
a wide range of musical instruments,

popular puppet shows, and famous
circus clowns, offer an unexpected
touch of color and festivity to the
museum's dark interior.

Witchcraft, clairvoyance, and
astrology, which were widespread in
both rural and urban France, are also
richly documented in this museum.
One of the most intriguing exhibits is
the cluttered, book-lined office of
Belline, a well-known Parisian
clairvoyant, which remained open
until 1974 on the Place Blanche.
Apart from the presence of tarot
cards, a crystal ball, a painting
of "The Third Eye," and a pair of
stuffed owls (a symbol of wisdom)
perched atop a bookcase, it might be
difficult to believe this innocuously
furnished office once belonged to a
psychic. "I wanted to dispel the false
idea that psychics operate in a fantastic world," Belline explains in the
museum's recorded interview.

With over 4,000 objects on display

in the cultural gallery and a total of
800,000 objects, documents, and
photographs in its collections, accessible to both scholars and the general
public, the Museum of Popular Arts
and Traditions performs a vital role in
recording and elucidating upon the
history of France and its people.

At the same time, because the
museum offers a rich documentation
of fundamental human activities, such
as the growing of food, the building
of houses, and the celebration of
holidays, visitors from all over are able
to better appreciate universal currents
of humanity in that all-encompassing
word: civilization.

A RE-ENACTMENT OF
FOUR SONS OF AYMON
FROM THE LILLE THEATER
OF LOUIS
AND GUSTAVE DE BUDT.

THIS PUNCHINELLO ONCE
HAD A STARRING ROLE
AT THE THÉÂTRE ANATOLE IN PARIS
DURING THE SECOND HALF
OF THE NINETEENTH CENTURY.

THE GOLD AND GREEN BRONZE-LIKE PATINA
ON THIS DECORATIVE BRASSWARE
IS THE RESULT OF A REMARKABLE SILVER-OXIDE PROCESS
INVENTED EARLY IN THE CENTURY THAT HAS
SINCE BEEN LOST.

Le Musée Bouilhet-Christofle
The Bouilhet-Christofle Museum

9, Rue Royale
75008 Paris
Tel: (01) 49–33–43–00

Visits by appointment only.

Metro: Concorde
Bus: 39, 48, 70, 89

UNTIL THE 1850s in France, people who weren't members of the aristocracy generally used cutlery made of iron or wood, and sometimes even ate with their hands. *Service à la française* (French table service) was the order of the day, limiting diners to eating from a single dish, and only those foods that were placed directly in front of them.

It took the marriage of Princess Mathilde Bonaparte, cousin of Emperor Napoléon III, to the Russian prince Anatoly Nikolaievich Demidoff, the Tsar's Ambassador in Paris, to initiate a major change in table service. It was because of him that *service à la russe* (Russian table service) came into vogue. With this style of dining, dishes were changed at least four to five times during the meal.

While the Russian nobility was creating a new fashion in dining, the triumphant bourgeoisie, which had made its fortune in trade and commerce, was discovering the art of gastronomy and elegant dining. But following the example of Guizot, Louis-Philippe's prime minister, who said: "Frenchmen, you will grow rich if you save!" this same bourgeoisie refused to spend huge sums on solid-silver tableware. A new type of silver-plating procedure that was being developed by an enterprising French-man was to correspond exactly to their need to impress, while still spending conservatively.

In addition to a fascinating over-view of the history of fine dining, visitors to the Bouilhet-Christofle Museum (which occupies the second floor of the former La Rochefoucauld

new procedure, and slowly began producing a broad assortment of dining accoutrements.

Keenly aware of the growth of railroads and maritime transportation, as well as the rise of tourism during the second half of the nineteenth century, the firm of Christofle rapidly made a name for itself as the leading purveyor of silver-plated commercial tableware, outfitting the dining cars on the Orient Express, luxurious *buffets de gare* (train station buffets) as far away as Odessa and Kiev, as well as hotel palaces such as the Negresco and the Martinez on the Côte d'Azur, and the Crillon, Ritz, and George V in Paris. The firm also produced customized silver-plated tableware for the first-class dining rooms of such luxury steamships as the *Normandie* (of 1882 and 1935) and the *Ile de France.*

"To my knowledge, this is the only museum devoted to the history of tableware from 1830 until the present time," explains its director, Henri Bouilhet. "During the nineteenth century, the way a table was set was part and parcel of social recognition and acceptance. My grandfather used to say that 'by buying Christofle, you could acquire a grandmother for little money.'

"With the rise of the great chefs, such as Escoffier, every dish was accompanied by the proper eating utensil. With this vast panoply of utensils, any mistakes in etiquette could be avoided."

Many of the silver-plated dining implements on display in this museum have fallen into disuse since the onslaught of microwaveable meals and take-out food. How many people use asparagus tongs for eating a single stalk at a time, leg-of-mutton sleeves for holding lamp chops, dainty scoopers for digging out lobster meat, or a chestnut warmer in the shape of

mansion on the Rue Royale), will discover to what extent a single man, Charles Christofle, was instrumental in the creation of a global industry in silver-plated tableware and home furnishings.

The son of a jeweler who specialized in making buttons of gold, mother-of-pearl, and silver, Christofle recognized the importance of a revolutionary technique known as "silver electroplating." This new procedure—perfected by Count Henri de Ruolz and two English silversmiths, George and Richard Elkington—was less onerous as well as less dangerous than the method that forced workers to inhale the fumes of heated mercury.

With the assistance of his wealthy brother-in-law, Joseph Bouilhet, Christofle bought the patents for this

a folded damask napkin? Still, they're so beautiful to look at, it's a shame they're no longer widely employed.

Only a discerning eye can tell the difference between a Christofle service of highly polished silver plate and one made of solid silver (the company made both). This new type of industrial process yielded such stunning silver-plate imitations that it wasn't long before Charles Christofle had caught the attention of King Louis Philippe and was appointed the official purveyor of his Château d'Eu, near Dieppe.

The Revolution of 1848 was to bring Christofle an even more important patron: Prince Louis-Napoléon Bonaparte. Eager to equal the splendor of his uncle Napoléon, Prince Louis ordered from Christofle a sumptuous set of gold-plated tableware for the Elysée Palace. Once he became Napoléon III, he commissioned the firm to equip all the imperial tables.

As purveyor to both a king and an emperor, Christofle was soon able to conquer foreign kingdoms as well, making tableware for the wealthy and well-born in the Kaiser's Germany, the Austro-Hungarian Empire, the Ottoman Empire, and the Russia of the Tsars.

Still, some rulers didn't just order tableware. One of the museum's recent acquisitions is the royal scepter and gavel of justice once belonging to the Haitian Emperor Faustin I. This former mulatto slave, who decreed himself emperor in 1844, commissioned Christofle to make him a Napoleonic scepter and gavel. (Faustin's empire was short-lived — he was killed less than twenty years later and Haiti became a republic.)

Christofle continues to furnish silver- and gold-plated tableware to the Elysée Palace, as well as to all the French ministries and embassies. With its strong ties to tradition, the French government still sets its table with the classic *Chinon* pattern, (also on display) that once graced the state dinners of Napoléon III.

After the death of Charles Christofle in 1863, his nephew Henri Bouilhet (great-grandfather of the museum's director) assumed the reins of the family business. It was at this time that the company received some notable architectural commissions thanks to a revolutionary process known as galvanoplasty, developed

THIS UNIQUE DECORATIVE SILVER BASIN, KNOWN AS *THE MINERVA*,
WAS CREATED BY CHARLES ROSSIGNEUX
FOR THE MARQUISE DE PAÏVA'S PRIVATE MANSION ON THE CHAMPS-ÉLYSÉES.
THE BOWL IS A COPY OF THE GALLO-ROMAN BASIN FROM THE HILDESHEIM COLLECTION,
NOW IN THE KUNSTHISTORISCHES MUSEUM IN VIENNA,
WHILE THE BASE WAS DESIGNED BY ROSSIGNEUX HIMSELF.

jointly by Bouilhet and Herman von Jacobi, a brilliant Russian inventor. A much more sophisticated type of electroplating, galvanoplasty made it possible to reproduce an exact though hollow replica of any object, regardless of its size or shape.

Consequently, Christofle was commissioned in 1869 to produce the monumental statue of the Virgin (ten meters in height) for the church Notre-Dame-de-la-Garde at the entrance to the port in Marseilles— still the world's largest example of galvanoplasty.

In 1875, the architect Charles Garnier commissioned the company to produce the groups of hollow winged statues in gilded bronze that now crown the cupola of the Opéra in Paris (a model of which is in the museum).

"Garnier relied on this process because the Opéra was being built on swampy terrain," Bouilhet explains. "If he were to put solid bronze statues on the roof, he knew that the building's foundations would sink into the ground. To prevent that from happening he decided to use hollow statues instead. The same principle would be applied to the Statue of Liberty."

But it turned out to be an eccentric Indian maharaja who, in 1878, commissioned the most outlandish object of all using galvanoplasty: a silver-plated and gilded wooden bed, decorated with the prince's monograms and coat of arms, whose corners were ornamented with four life-size hollow bronze nudes painted in flesh tones, with real hair and moveable eyes.

An unsigned watercolor of this unique bed now hangs in the museum, showing the four types of women the maharaja wanted by his bedside: Parisian, Spanish, Italian, and Greek. Each figure holds a fan intended to chase flies away when the occupant was in bed.

While the museum has objects that reflect a playful element, the collection as a whole represents the consummate *bon goût* of the company's designers and craftsmen, as well as a long-standing appreciation of trends in art and design—a sensibility that continues to this day. Japonisme, Naturalism, Art Nouveau, and Art Deco were among the art movements that inspired some of the company's most innovative designs, many of which are handsomely displayed and labeled in both French and English in the museum's vitrines.

Among the numerous artistic luminaries who have worked with the company since its founding are: Albert Carrier-Belleuse, Jean-Baptiste Carpeaux, Jean Cocteau, and Jean-Michel Folon.

Bouilhet credits the advent of the Universal Expositions, "the great social and cultural events of the nineteenth century," as inspiring Christofle to outdo itself in terms of both technical and artistic innovation.

While many of the designs in this museum are one-of-a-kind objects that will most likely never be produced again, Bouilhet refuses to believe that they have only a nostalgic value.

"To me, this museum is not just for visitors to see how people lived and ate in the past. It is also a conservatory, a place of ideas from which designers and craftsmen can still draw inspiration." Judging by the splendid and fascinating contents of this museum, those who visit it will agree wholeheartedly.

THIS OUTSTANDING THREE-AND-ONE-HALF-FOOT-HIGH TEA FOUNTAIN
WAS FEATURED AT THE UNIVERSAL EXPOSITION OF VIENNA IN 1873.

Le Musée National de la Céramique
The National Museum of Ceramics

Place de la Manufacture
92310 Sèvres
Tel: (01) 41-14-04-20

Open from 10:00 A.M. to 5:00 P.M. every day except Tuesday and holidays.

Metro: Pont de Sèvres. Take the bridge across the Seine, either by Bus (169, 171, 179) or on foot.

THE EDIFICE OF THE NATIONAL MUSEUM OF CERAMICS, WAS CONCEIVED BY THE ARCHITECT ALEXANDRE LAUDIN.

VISITORS TO THIS unique museum overlooking the Seine are surprised to discover a splendid group of reproductions of some of the world's greatest masterpieces from the Louvre and the Vatican Museums, including Titian's *Portrait of Flora*, Jean-Antoine Watteau's *Embarkation for Cythera*, Raphael's *Deliverance of St. Peter*, Tintoretto's *Portrait of Man*, and Sir Anthony van Dyck's *Self-Portrait*. They are even more astonished to learn that they were painted on sheets of porcelain at the Manufactory of Sèvres between 1825 and 1850.

These extraordinary pieces represent only a fraction of the riches on display at the National Museum of Ceramics, reputedly the world's largest and oldest museum dedicated to the ceramic arts. Its rich and

A SEVENTEENTH-CENTURY
ENAMELED DECORATIVE PLATE
WITH MOLDED
REPTILES, PLANTS, AND SHELLS,
FROM THE SCHOOL OF
BERNARD PALISSY.

unparalleled collection is largely a product of the diligence and initiative of Alexandre Brongniart, the head of the Manufactory of Sèvres from 1800 until his death in 1847. The son of the architect and scientist, Théodore Brongniart, who designed the Bourse (the Paris Stock Exchange), Alexandre wrote what has come to be considered a sort of bible on the technology of ceramics: *Treatise on the Ceramic Arts,* published between 1841 and 1844. In order to complete his research for this work, he purchased many pieces of stoneware from all over the world, and was given even more (often in exchange for Sèvres porcelain).

He also appointed Désiré Riocreux, one of the factory's decorators, to oversee the exhaustive collections at the Museum of Ceramics and Glass, which was inaugurated in 1824 next to the factory in Sèvres's center. (Riocreux held the post of museum curator for nearly five decades, until his death in 1872!) Together, both men made a fundamental decision to classify the collections according to different technical processes—a system of classification still in use today.

In 1876, the Sèvres factory and museum were moved to their current premises on a hill south of the Seine between the Sèvres Bridge and the Saint-Cloud Park, below the famous Breteuil pavilion housing the standard meter and kilo. At the entrance to the museum is a weathered bronze statue of one of France's greatest ceramicists, Bernard Palissy (c. 1510–c. 1589), noted for his smooth glazes in richly colored enamels and his rustic ceramics decorated with amazingly life-like reptiles, shells, and plants.

THIS BLUE-AND-WHITE FAÏENCE STOVE WAS MADE IN STRASBOURG
BY FRANÇOIS-PAUL ACKER C. 1735;
THE STOVE'S DECORATIVE PANELS DEPICT VARIOUS RURAL
ACTIVITIES COMMON TO THE REGION.

The word "ceramics" comes from the Greek *keramos*, meaning clay, and includes any type of baked pottery that has undergone an irreversible physical-chemical change, including glazed and unglazed pottery, stoneware, faïence, and porcelain.

Although the two-story museum contains several informative vitrines on different ceramic techniques, it is the extensive series of displays demonstrating the international development of this decorative art that captures the imagination. The depth and range of the collection are staggering; only about half of the museum's 100,000 pieces can be shown at any one time because of a lack of space.

Among the sights to behold are red and black ancient Greek terra-cotta vases and amphorae fashioned fourteen centuries before the birth of Christ, sixteenth-century lead-glazed terra-cotta rustic roof ornaments from Beauvais, France, rare blue-and-white Dutch Delftware, life-size animals made of white Meissen porcelain, a jardinière filled with a bouquet of exquisite soft-paste porcelain flowers from Vincennes, and highly ornate vases and amphorae from Sèvres, whose porcelain embellishments could easily be mistaken for gold.

No other museum in Paris can claim such a rich collection of Islamic ceramics, whose technique was eventually transmitted throughout Western Europe, via Spain and Italy. Two rooms on the ground floor illustrate the evolution of the Muslim world's tin-glaze faïence and luster-ware—both of which were invented and perfected in the eighth and ninth centuries—as well as that of siliceous pottery, prized for its turquoise glaze, yet unknown in the West until 1750. Not to be overlooked is the outstanding group of sixteenth- and

THIS UNUSUAL TABLE PEDESTAL,
ATTRIBUTED TO GIUSEPPE GERCCI,
IS A SUPERB EXAMPLE OF
EIGHTEENTH-CENTURY ITALIAN
SOFT-PASTE PORCELAIN
MADE IN CAPODIMONTE, NAPLES.
C. 1756–58.

seventeenth-century Iznik ceramics, famed for their vivid blue, turquoise, and coral-red floral designs, and a rare collection of fifteenth-century Hispano-Moresque gold and cream-colored lusterware from Malaga, Valencia, and Manisa.

The museum's faïence from the Italian Renaissance is notable for both its quality and quantity, thus offering the visitor a comprehensive overview of its development. Faïence was invented as a substitute for Chinese porcelain which, because it had to be imported, was far more rare and costly. Made of common clay, the faïence was then covered with white enamel and baked at a temperature of 800 to 900 degrees Celsius.

Although faïence first appeared in Spain during the fourteenth century, this ceramic art only began to flourish in Tuscany during the fifteenth century. It attained new heights in Faenza in the sixteenth century (which spawned the French term *faïence*), with the usage of polychrome designs and *istoriato* (chronicles), which were reproductions of period engravings. Among the museum's rarities is a 1525 dish with a vivid depiction of the Biblical story *Joseph Finding the Bowl Hidden in Benjamin's Bag*, stamped "Casa Pirota," the most renowned factory in Faenza.

While some artists were content to decorate faïence plates with religious and genre scenes for such important patrons as the Medici popes, others, such as the Della Robbia sculptors in Florence, used this lustrous white ceramic to make altarpieces, decorative bas-reliefs, and even sculptures. One of them, Girolamo della Robbia, came to France in 1527–28 to work under King Francis I. A profoundly moving life-size faïence statue of *A Madonna and Child*, which dominates a corner of the museum's ground floor, is attributed to him.

Visitors shouldn't miss the superb reconstruction of a seventeenth-century apothecary, which contains hundreds of sixteenth- and seventeenth-century faïence jars of diverse shapes and origins that once held liquid elixirs and dried medicines (as well as placebos).

Although the highly prized hard-paste porcelain created with the white clay kaolin was being made in China in the seventh and eighth centuries of our era (the word "porcelain" comes from the word for the pig-shaped cowrie shell, *porcello*), it was not until the eighteenth century that Europeans found the means to produce the same type of coveted stoneware.

Still, by the sixteenth century, the Medici court in Florence was promoting the production of soft-paste

A MADONNA AND CHILD, FROM THE ATELIER OF GIROLAMO DELLA ROBBIA, IN THE NATIONAL MUSEUM OF CERAMICS.

THIS SWEEPING STONE STAIRCASE LEADS TO
A DAZZLING GALLERY OF OLD MASTER REPRODUCTIONS
PAINTED ON PORCELAIN PLAQUES.

THIS MAGNIFICENT JARDINIÈRE
BRIMMING OVER WITH
PORCELAIN BLOOMS
WAS MADE AT VINCENNES
IN 1750–51.

porcelain—one made without kaolin and therefore easily marred. The museum's most valuable objects are its group of blue and white "Medici" porcelains, regarded as the earliest ones made in Europe. Notable among them is a blue bottle in the shape of a grotesque face and two blue-and-white flasks embellished with the arms of Philip II of Spain.

In 1708 the first European hard-paste porcelain was produced by Meissen ceramicists in Saxony. In the meantime, the French had discovered a way to make translucent, soft-paste porcelain without kaolin, a process that would be short-lived due to its high risk of imperfections during the kilning process. So prized was this porcelain, that King Louis XV (at the behest of his mistress Madame de Pompadour), took an active interest in the factory's production at Vincennes. Later, after its move to Sèvres in 1756, the King re-named it the Royal Manufactory of Sèvres.

The museum's extensive group of soft-paste porcelains reflects the epoch's fascination with the Rococo and *Chinoiserie*. Among the most outstanding pieces is an exquisite soft-paste porcelain ewer with matching basin, made in Vincennes (c. 1753), whose lapis-lazuli ground obtained from cobalt oxide would soon be known as the famous *bleu de Sèvres*, after the factory was moved.

The discovery of an important vein of kaolin at Saint-Yrieux-la-Perche near Limoges in 1768, inspired a new generation of artists at Sèvres to begin making unusual objects out of hard-paste porcelain, whose resistance and durability permitted greater experimentation with shape and color. Finding inspiration from Greco-Roman antiquity with the discovery of the ruins of Pompeii and Herculaneum, they executed many models in the Neoclassical mode,

including *bol-seins* (breasted bowls) for Marie-Antoinette's dairy at the Château of Rambouillet. This flesh-colored, breast-shaped drinking bowl, which is set on a porcelain tripod made of three mythical rams, is in a class by itself.

It was during the aegis of Alexandre Brongniart that the Manufactory of Sèvres reached its apogee in terms of technical prowess, showing that the art of porcelain could take its rightful place with other arts, including painting, cabinetwork, and metalwork. Nowhere is this mastery more evident than in the stunning porcelain, wood, and gilded bronze *Secretary of the Muses*, where the trompe-l'oeil designs on porcelain emulate both bronze plaques and carved cameos.

The multiple types of stoneware on display at the National Museum of Ceramics encourage an entirely new awareness and appreciation of this often overlooked decorative art. Today, the world is indebted to Alexandre Brongniart, whose passionate interest in the aesthetics and technology of ceramics laid the groundwork for this uniquely impressive museum.

Le Musée Cernuschi

The Cernuschi Museum

7, Avenue Vélasquez
75008 Paris
Tel: (01) 45-63-50-75

**Open Tuesday through Sunday
10:00 A.M. to 5:40 P.M.**

**Metro: Villiers, Monceau
Bus: 30, 94**

Of THE THOUSANDS of people who frequent the Parc Monceau in Paris, few realize that an elegant white stone mansion at the edge of the park, built in the 1870s, now houses one of the most impressive collections of ancient Chinese art in Europe. Known as the Cernuschi Museum, it was left to the City of Paris one hundred years ago, by the wealthy Milanese financier and philanthropist Henri Cernuschi (1820–1896).

Today, only certain art connoisseurs know that Cernuschi was one of the first collectors in France to have the aesthetic discernment to amass an important collection of Chinese and Japanese art. An atypical amalgam of innovative tycoon and romantic revolutionary, Cernuschi became a serious collector partly through a series of inauspicious circumstances. As a prominent sympathizer with the insurgents of the 1871 Commune, he was arrested, albeit briefly, and then released. Deeply shocked and horrified by the wave of people (some of whom were his friends) who were killed or imprisoned during this bloody popular uprising, in September 1871 he embarked upon an eighteen-month voyage around the world that would take him to China and Asia by way of America.

Accompanying him on this trip was the noted critic Théodore Duret (1838–1927), a staunch friend and advocate of the Impressionists, and an ardent admirer of Japanese art. Duret's fellowship proved decisive, since his expertise in Oriental art influenced many of Cernuschi's acquisitions. Still, the Milanese financier

THE BARBARIAN TRIBUTE BEARER.
TERRA-COTTA WITH CREAM GLAZE, RETOUCHED WITH PAINT.
TANG DYNASTY.

was sufficiently knowledgeable to be both a discerning and enthusiastic buyer in his own right. "Cernuschi had taste and didn't lack for money," Duret recalled in his memoirs. "With impudent pleasure, he carried off a whole cargo load of Chinese and Japanese porcelain vases, sculpted wood pieces, lacquers, ceramics, bronzes, ivories . . . , showing a preference for the most ancient objects, whose art, by its very originality, had captivated him."

The largest piece Cernuschi acquired on his trip was the *Great Buddha of Meguro*, a giant seventeenth-century bronze deity from the Meguro Temple in Tokyo, which had been destroyed in a fire. This awesome effigy, impressively displayed on a raised platform overlooking a vast gallery on the museum's second floor, was shipped in pieces and then resoldered in Paris by Emile Gustave Leblanc Barbédienne, who cast many of Rodin's bronzes.

One of Cernuschi's most unusual and obscure acquisitions was a mammoth ancient molded bronze basin from the Warring States period (475 B.C.–221 B.C.), referred to as a *kien* or "mirror," presumably because the water inside it reflected the light from nocturnal ceremonial torches. Displayed prominently on the museum's ground floor, it remains the largest known Chinese basin from that period.

In the mid-1870s, Cernuschi commissioned the architect Bouwens to build a three-story mansion next to the Parc Monceau, with a special gallery spacious enough to accommodate the Meguro Buddha and the other objects he had brought back from the Far East.

Although his mansion and splendid Oriental collections were willed to the City of Paris, with the clear proviso that a museum should be created, his

THIS FUNERARY STELE
FROM THE NORTHERN QI DYNASTY
SHOWS A BUDDHA
SURROUNDED BY HIS DISCIPLES.

testament granted the city a free hand in the running of the institution. This absence of a restrictive clause made it possible for the museum's first curator, Henri d'Ardenne de Tizac, to reorient the museum's collections toward objects from ancient China, which were just being discovered. Today, visitors to the Cernuschi Museum will be impressed by its exceptional collection of Chinese art and objects dating as far back as the Neolithic period before the birth of China and extending to the Song dynasty (A.D. 960–A.D. 1279). The museum also has a fine collection of over 200 twentieth-century Chinese scroll paintings using the traditional technique of ink on paper from both Taiwan and mainland China, the largest of its kind on the Continent. "In terms of quality, the Cernuschi is considered to rank high among the most important museums of Chinese art in Europe," notes curator Gilles Béguin.

The mansion's interior has been significantly altered since Cernuschi's death. Apart from the stately gated entrance, flanked by two fantastic Chinese bronze lions, and the lobby's pristine white and burgundy mosaic tile floor, little remains of the mansion's former exotic splendor. Between 1932 and 1960, two curators, René Grousset and Vadime Eliseeff, modernized the museum's ground floor, where the permanent collection is kept, and the second floor, now used for temporary exhibitions of art from China, Japan, and Korea. Most of the 1,000 pieces on display—with the exception of the large sculptures and bronzes—are simply presented and identified in well-lit vitrines. Both connoisseurs and amateurs of Oriental art appreciate the Cernuschi Museum's relative anonymity and spare decor, which provide an atmosphere conducive to quiet contemplation and aesthetic appreciation.

The museum's undisputed masterpiece of early bronze art is "The Tigress," a rather elaborate lidded jug in the form of a kneeling feline, its open jaws protecting an ancestor of the clan. Fashioned in Anyang (then China's capital) in the Hunan province at the end of the Shang dynasty (1600 B.C.–1100 B.C), the jug is a marvel of imaginative artistry: while the front represents a mythical tiger holding beneath its menacing jaws a small figure notable for the astonished expression on its face, the rear is set off by a tail that doubles as an elephant's trunk, and raised designs that constitute the animal's features.

THIS *YEOU* VASE, KNOWN AS
"LA TIGRESSE" (THE TIGRESS),
A BRONZE RITUAL VESSEL USED FOR
SERVING GRAIN ALCOHOL,
WAS MADE DURING THE END OF THE
SHANG DYNASTY.

"This jug was presumably used to hold a delicate alcohol made from barley, which was served hot," notes Béguin. "The spoon that once went with it has long since disappeared. There are only two known bronzes in the world like it; one is in our museum and the other is in Japan."

The oldest objects in the museum are some surprisingly flat and smooth rectangular stone axes, simple hand-painted terra-cotta vessels (including a *Ma-kia-yao* vase that goes back 3,000 years B.C.), and a strange tripod cooking vessel made of gray clay resembling three mammaries that have been soldered together.

The Oriental notion of serenity is especially evident in two of the museum's stone Buddhist sculptures: the *Kouan-yin with Gourd* from the Sui dynasty (A.D. 581–A.D. 618), an arresting Bodhisattva, with half-closed eyes, an enigmatic smile and evanescent robes embellished with delicate stone ribbons and jewels; and a funerary stele from the Northern Qi dynasty (A.D. 550–A.D. 577), depicting a Buddha surrounded by his disciples, a landmark in symmetry and majesty.

As was true of the Egyptians, the Chinese had a tradition of burying their dead with small figurines— *ming-k'i*—believing that these objects repelled evil spirits. The museum has an extensive collection of these figurines, which were generally made of glazed and unglazed terra-cotta or wood, some of them dating as far back as the Han dynasty (206 B.C.– A.D. 220). Most of the statuettes are simplified, lively facsimiles of witches, women, and children, as well as of such domesticated animals as dogs, goats, oxen, and pigs. A charmingly naturalistic white glazed terra-cotta Chinese pug dog, from the Han period, portrayed waiting with his ears pricked up and an alert gaze, demonstrates the artist's acute powers of observation.

The museum's most outstanding porcelains, funerary figurines, as well as its famous painted scroll *Horses and Grooms*, attributed to Han Kan, one of China's greatest court painters, are ascribed to the Tang dynasty (A.D. 618–A.D. 907), considered China's Golden Age. The Tang rulers saw themselves as the leaders of the greatest empire under the sky; their capital, Chang-an, was the largest walled city ever built. So great was the wealth of this period, that edicts were passed regulating the number of figurines that could be buried with

SPLENDIDLY DECKED OUT IN RED FLAGS
FOR A SPECIAL EXHIBIT, THE *GREAT BUDDHA OF MEGURO*
PRESIDES OVER THE PRECIOUS COLLECTION
AT THE CERNUSCHI MUSEUM.

the dead, which sometimes numbered in the hundreds.

One of the most profoundly stirring pieces from this period is a legless wooden horse, notable for its finely sculpted body, bowed head, half-open mouth and carefully carved fringe of hair above its eyes. Not only is this a piece of exceptional beauty and rarity, but it is the only known wooden horse sculpture from the Tang era outside of China.

The famous Silk Route, between China and the eastern part of the Mediterranean, is also represented at the museum through small terra-cotta sculptures of caravanners, bearded merchants, and camels laden with goods. One of the most remarkable

figurines illustrating this era of trade and outside exchange is *The Barbarian Tribute Bearer* made of glazed terra-cotta and painted in delicate shades of green, pink, black, and blue. With his prominent pro-truding eyes, fur-trimmed cap and costume, and closely clasped horn of plenty, he exudes a fetching *joie de vivre* that seems to transcend space and time.

This unique figure, which dates back to the seventh century of our era, appears as a messenger of peace and abundance. It is appealing to think of him as the happy harbinger of the riches awaiting visitors who have the good fortune to discover this elegant and enthralling museum.

Le Musée Cognacq-Jay

The Cognacq-Jay Museum

8, Rue Elzévir
75003 Paris
Tel: (01) 40–27–07–21

Open Tuesday through Sunday
10:00 A.M. to 5:40 P.M.
Closed Mondays and holidays

Metro: Saint Paul
Bus: 29, 69, 76, 96

THE FAÇADE
OF THE MUSÉE COGNACQ-JAY
REFLECTS THE
LATE-SIXTEENTH-CENTURY
ARCHITECTURAL STYLE
OF PHILIBERT DE L'ORME.

ON A QUIET, narrow street in the Marais, behind massive portals once reserved for horse-drawn carriages, is a magnificently restored Parisian mansion, the Hôtel Donon, built and modified during the reigns of Henry II and his three sons. The mansion was constructed at the end of the sixteenth century for Médéric de Donon, counselor to the king and superintendent of buildings, as well as husband to Jeanne della Robbia, grand-daughter of the Florentine sculptor, Andrea della Robbia.

After centuries of neglect, the City of Paris has transformed this once dilapidated dwelling into the stunning Cognacq-Jay Museum, which has been open to the public since the end of 1990. It is both a surprise and a pleasure to discover that behind this building's sober façade there is a sumptuously furnished interior suggesting the *mode de vie* of an accomplished and sophisticated eighteenth-century French bourgeois household. The museum is a triumph of restoration, with its period *boiseries,* time-worn black-and-white stone floors, Aubusson carpets and modern recessed lighting, marrying the atmosphere of an elegant private home with the modern conveniences of a public exhibition space.

Seeing the airy white and gold paneled Leszczynska Room on the first floor with its Louis XV furniture, views of Venice by Canaletto, portraits of Queen Marie Leszczynska and two of the famous sisters Nesle (both mistresses to Louis XV) by Jean-Marc Nattier, it's easy to imagine how this might have been a *salon* where luminaries of the French

THE LESZCZYNSKA ROOM, WHOSE EIGHTEENTH-CENTURY WHITE AND GOLD PANELING,
FOUR DOORS, AND WINDOWS ARE PART OF THE ORIGINAL MANSION,
HAS A COMPLETE COLLECTION OF CONVERSATION CHAIRS BY JEAN-BAPTISTE LELARGE (1743–1802)
ADORNED WITH CORNFLOWER-PATTERNED BEAUVAIS TAPESTRIES AND
TWO EXCEPTIONAL LIGHT TABLES, ATTRIBUTED TO JEAN-FRANÇOIS OEBEN (1720–1763).
ONE OF THESE RARE TABLES, WITH ITS CHINTZ FLOWER MARQUETRY AND SLIDING TRAY REVEALING
A SECRET DRAWER, IS SAID TO HAVE BEEN COMMISSIONED BY MADAME DE POMPADOUR.

THIS *ROCAILLE* SALON WITH ITS MAGNIFICENT
EIGHTEENTH-CENTURY OAK PANELING
CONTAINS LOUIS XVI FURNISHINGS AND A 1789 PASTEL,
MISS POWER, BY JOHN RUSSELL (1745–1806),
ONE OF ENGLAND'S FOREMOST PASTELISTS.
THE TURQUOISE SÈVRES PORCELAIN CLOCK (ONE OF A PAIR)
IS BY PIERRE GOUTHIÈRE (1732–1813).

Enlightenment would meet to discuss the latest works by Rousseau or Buffon.

The Cognacq-Jay Museum is noteworthy for the way in which it manages to convey a feeling of intimacy, while providing a comprehensive presentation of eighteenth-century painting, drawing, sculpture, and applied arts, including Meissen figurines, finely crafted jeweled and enameled snuffboxes and *nécessaires* (toiletry and sewing kits)—exquisite vestiges of an era that would culminate in the French Revolution.

Visitors will be enchanted by such rarities as the wooden inlay table once owned by Madame de Pompadour, a magnificent bronze and ebony desk decorated with copper and mother-of-pearl inlay, as well as by the gorgeous cerulean silk brocade canopy bed once slept in by Louis XVI's aunt, Madame Adélaïde. Equally impressive are the museum's picture and sculpture galleries filled with carefully chosen works by Chardin, Watteau, Tiepolo, Van Ruysdaël, Fragonard, Boucher, Vigée Lebrun, Greuze, Falconet, Houdon, Clodion, Reynolds, Lawrence, and Rembrandt.

There are a myriad of treasures to discover at this museum, including a room filled with masterful pastel portraits by one of the greatest practitioners of the medium, Maurice-Quentin de La Tour. It's hard to forget his insightful portrait of *La Présidente de Rieux Dressed for a Ball*, sumptuously outfitted in gray silk lavishly ornamented with yards of teal-blue taffeta ribbon.

The Oval Room is another small jewel: painted in tones of pale turquoise, it features five affecting children's portraits by Jean-Baptiste Greuze, vitrines filled with finely painted Sèvres porcelains, and exquisitely carved crystal and amethyst chalices, as well as two sensuous marble statues: *Venus Holding Her Chariot's Reins* by François-Marie Poncet and *Child with Bird* by Jean-Baptiste Pigalle.

There are over 1,000 objects on display at the Cognacq-Jay Museum, spread over four floors, and a leisurely visit takes the better part of an afternoon. The museum's effective amalgam of grandeur and delicacy, coupled with the breadth of its collections, make it unique among Parisian institutions.

"The Cognacq-Jay museum is an exceptional collection because it's an assembly of objects brought together by a single person from a given moment of civilization," notes curator Pascal de la Vaissière. "It imparts an appreciation of all the techniques in art which attained a certain excellence in the eighteenth century."

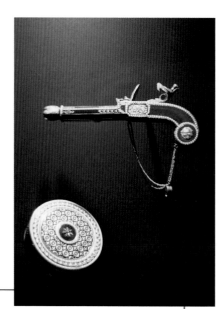

THIS GOLD AND ENAMEL FRENCH SNUFFBOX, AND THE GOLD AND RED ENAMEL PERFUME VIAL SHAPED LIKE A PISTOL ARE REPRESENTATIVE OF THE MUSEUM'S COLLECTION OF EXQUISITE EIGHTEENTH- AND NINETEENTH-CENTURY PRECIOUS SMALL OBJECTS.

THIS LARGE EBONY-PLATED DESK,
INLAID WITH BRASS, COPPER,
MOTHER-OF-PEARL, GREEN AND RED HORN,
AND RICHLY ADORNED WITH GILT BRONZE,
IS IN THE OLD MASTERS GALLERY. C. 1725.
ATOP THE DESK IS THE MARBLE SCULPTURE
*CHILD WITH A RAISED GOBLET IN
BACCHUS'S RETINUE*
BY J. C. VASSE. C. 1750.

Ernest Cognacq, the "single person" who assembled these stunning eighteenth-century artworks and furnishings with the tacit approval of his spouse, Marie-Louise Jay (the museum is named after the couple), was as remarkable as the collection itself.

Born into a modest household in 1839 at Saint-Martin-de-Ré in the French Alps, Cognacq was orphaned at the age of eleven and forced to leave school to earn his livelihood in Paris. Eventually, he became a dry-goods peddler on the Pont Neuf, the city's oldest bridge. The site exerted an influence upon Cognacq and, in 1872, he opened a small shop in a café near the Pont Neuf, calling it La Samaritaine. It was to be the precursor of one of Paris's largest department stores, which first opened its doors in 1900.

By 1925, this self-made entrepreneur was running a retail empire with annual sales in excess of a billion francs, and had turned over sixty-five percent of the company's profits to its employees. His greatest pleasure was spending his hard-earned fortune on magnificent works of art, which have been compared with those in the Wallace Collection at Hertford House in London, a museum that Cognacq both envied and admired.

In light of his modest beginnings and consuming business activities, it might seem unusual that Ernest Cognacq should possess such a heightened aesthetic sense. Yves Sevy, a journalist who knew Cognacq, wrote after his death: "His humble beginnings did not particularly predispose him to love beautiful things. But, in fact, he had very profound instincts, a real passion for that which was beautiful and superb."

Moreover, Cognacq was an innovator and independent thinker by nature. He proved no different in his approach to the arts. He collected English painting before it was fashionable, including works by masters who were little known at the time. Some of the paintings that he chose hang in the museum's English Gallery, including a beautiful full-length portrait of *Mrs. Lloyd* by Sir Joshua Reynolds, a study for *Head of Young Woman with Loosened Hair* by George Romney, and a portrait of the *Princess Metternich* by Sir Thomas Lawrence.

Still, as passionate as he was about art, Cognacq was also honest enough to acknowledge his limitations. At the celebrated 1902 Desfossés auction he confided to the future Petit Palais

THE LOUIS XVI CHAMBER IS DOMINATED BY A SPLENDID CANOPIED BED
À LA POLONAISE, WHICH IS THOUGHT TO HAVE BEEN COMMISSIONED
BY VAUDREUIL (A CLOSE FRIEND OF MARIE-ANTOINETTE)
AND BOUGHT BACK BY THE CROWN FOR THE KING'S AUNT, MADAME ADÉLAÏDE,
WHEN VAUDREUIL WENT BANKRUPT.
THE SILK COVER WAS REWOVEN FROM THE ORIGINAL MODEL.

curator Camille Gronkowski: "I came here to buy a few paintings but I don't know much and don't see well. Would you give me a few ideas?" The twenty-six-year-old Gronkowski offered his opinion, and to his great amazement, watched Cognacq buy exactly what he had advised. That fortuitous meeting was the beginning of a long friendship, as well as a fruitful collaboration.

Still, there was no one upon whom he relied more than Edouard Jonas (1883–1961) to help him accumulate the bulk of his collection. Jonas, who was both a Socialist and a well-established art dealer, was the antithesis of the stolid, retiring Cognacq. As the owner of two prominent art galleries, one in Paris, the other in New York, he eventually became Cognacq's principal adviser as well as an important resource for drawings, paintings, sculpture, furniture, and bibelots. It was Jonas who would help Cognacq acquire drawings by Watteau and Ingres, portraits by Jean-Baptiste Greuze, pastels by Maurice-Quentin de La Tour, as well as many charming minor works depicting eighteenth-century bourgeois life by Jean-Baptiste Mallet, François Dumont, and Philibert-Louis Debucourt.

In 1925, Cognacq turned eighty-six. That same year he did the unthinkable: with the guidance and assistance of Jonas, he set aside a limited area for temporary displays from his collection inside the Samaritaine de Luxe on the Boulevard des Capucines. His ambition: to heighten the general public's awareness of what he considered to be the finest examples of the visual arts. It was the first time customers had a chance to view an original Chardin and a La Tour inside a department store.

These temporary exhibitions were so well received that Cognacq decided to create a three-story museum in a building adjacent to the Samaritaine on the Boulevard des Capucines, which he bequeathed to the City of Paris upon his death. Unfortunately, Cognacq never lived to see his last wish fulfilled; he died in February 1928 while his collection was being installed.

Inaugurated by France's President Paul Doumer in 1929, this museum remained open to the public until 1986, when the collection was transferred to the Hôtel Donon. A visit to the Cognacq-Jay Museum today only serves to reaffirm what Eugène Jolas is remembered as saying when the collection was unveiled to the public in 1929:

"Ernest Cognacq had unfailing taste, so that when he came upon a rare masterpiece and acquired it, he would contemplate and caress it with great satisfaction. His hand would often linger over the contours of an antique table or a rare chest; he had the true pleasure that is only known to amateurs." Now, we too can share in that pleasure.

THIS BOWL IN *PÂTE DE RIZ*
(WHITE AGATE GLASS)
WITH OPAL GREEN HANDLES SHAPED LIKE SINUOUS SNAKES
IS MOUNTED ON AN ALABASTER BASE. 1855.
(COURTESY MUSÉE DE CRISTAL DE BACCARAT.)

Le Musée de Cristal de Baccarat

The Museum of Baccarat Crystal

30 bis, Rue du Paradis
75010 Paris
Tel: (01) 47–70–64–30

Open Monday through Saturday
9:00 A.M. to 6:00 P.M.

Metro: Poissonnière, Gare de l'Est
Bus: 32

IN 1832, the heads of Baccarat and Saint-Louis, the two leading crystal producers in France, established a sales office with two wholesalers inside a former posthouse at 30, Rue du Paradis Poissonnière. Little did these men realize that their practical business decision would have such lasting consequences—today, the same building, albeit greatly changed, accommodates Baccarat's international headquarters and its recently remodeled museum. While the name of the street has been abbreviated to Paradis, and the area has altered significantly over the course of 164 years, the reputation of Baccarat has remained constant, being synonymous with the finest in luxury crystal throughout the world.

The Museum of Baccarat Crystal is located on the building's second floor at the top of an imposing flight of red-carpeted oak stairs. Visitors are often amused by the sight of "Dame Baccarat," a plaster mannequin near the museum entrance, festooned in a glittering "gown" of crystal drops.

Bedecked with an extraordinary pair of matching crystal and bronze 1840 chandeliers over two meters high, the museum's main gallery displays a collection of rare crystal glassware, perfume bottles, and decorative objects, many of which are stunning works of art. The visitor will also walk through two ornately decorated Belle Epoque rooms furnished with damask-covered tables set with intricately cut crystal dishes, glasses, and candelabra, illustrating the evolution of elegant French dining. Easy-to-read, informative panels spanning three centuries describe the history of

THIS AUTHENTIC
BELLE EPOQUE DINING ROOM
DISPLAYS A STUNNING
TABLE OF ANTIQUE BACCARAT
CRYSTAL.

crystal and Baccarat within the context of major historical events that helped shape the company's fortunes, as well as the way people lived.

"Our aim with this museum is to show how a single enterprise was linked to society and sociology, as well as to the *art de vivre*," notes curator Dany Sautot. "At the same time, this museum is about the history of taste and styles."

France is indebted to England for the discovery of lead crystal. In 1676, after various experiments, the English glass industrialist George Ravenscroft had the idea of adding lead oxide to the original glass compound to assure a clear, colorless glass. Even though his experiment failed to yield the clarity, sparkle, and sound of crystal as we know it today, it did give birth to the first lead-based product.

From the end of the seventeenth century onward, this crystal was improved through the use of better and more purified raw materials. People were delighted by the way candlelight caused this new type of glassware to shimmer, and it wasn't long before British lead crystal spread throughout Europe, North America, and India.

By the second half of the eighteenth century, wine glasses with a funneled bowl, connected to a solid base by a straight stem, began to make their appearance. It was also at this time that crystal light fixtures were introduced, and soon the formerly dark interiors of palaces and wealthy homes were aglow with the brilliant light of chandeliers.

Despite the continuous conflicts that divided England and France, this development in glassware appealed to the Gallic sense of refinement, and the French were soon imitating English crystal. In 1760, the French King Louis XV granted the Bishopric of Metz permission to open the Sainte-Anne Glassworks in Baccarat, a small town fifty kilometers from Nancy on the right bank of the Meurthe River. Although the Baccarat glassworks prospered until 1789, the advent of the French Revolution and the subsequent Napoleonic Wars proved disastrous to the company— by 1816 it had been forced into bankruptcy.

Nonetheless, two major events were to alter Baccarat's destiny: the defeat of Napoléon at Waterloo in 1815 and the redrawing of the map of Europe after the Empire's dismantling.

The resulting diplomatic treaties now put the former French department of Sambre and Meuse in Belgium, an event that was to have a substantial impact upon the region's leading crystal producer, the Vonêche Crystalworks, owned by Aimé-Gabriel d'Artigues, an eminent specialist in the field. Overnight, when the Vonêche plant was declared to be on Belgian rather than French soil, d'Artigues was faced with a dual problem: high customs duties along the newly drawn borders and heavy competition from English lead crystal manufacturers. Fortunately, the industrious d'Artigues contrived a clever solution to his dilemma: if he could be allowed to import his crystalware into France without paying duties for two years, he would cut and engrave it in a factory that he would personally establish on French soil. The new French King Louis XVIII, anxious to revive this growth industry, assented to this novel proposition. Consequently, in 1816, d'Artigues acquired the former Sainte-Anne Glassworks in Baccarat.

By then, crystal was all the rage. Whereas, under the Old Régime, drinking glasses were not permitted on the table but were brought in by servants, after the Restoration the best houses provided each dinner guest with a water glass, two glasses for wine (one for red, one for white), and a flute glass for champagne—a form of etiquette that is observed to this day. While Baccarat's great period began with d'Artigues, his association with the company was brief: by 1823, ill health and financial difficulties had forced him to sell his plant.

The new company that emerged from the sale, the *Compagnie des Verreries et Cristalleries de Vonêche Baccarat* was directed by Pierre-Antoine Godard-Desmarest, who established the company credo: "Perfection"—one which was to apply both to the quality of his crystal and to his labor force.

Within five years of its inception, the company had gained an important foothold in the French market. Baccarat's reputation was such that, by 1828, the French King Charles X visited the factory in the pouring rain: in honor of this momentous event, the monarch was presented with a lavishly engraved crystal ewer with the French royal coat of arms enameled on gold and inlaid in the crystal (now part of the museum's collection).

Baccarat justly earned its reputation for tireless creativity. By the mid-1840s, thanks to improvements in the process of making colored, non-reflective glass by François-Eugène de Fontenay, the company became a leader in manufacturing

"agate glass," a milky translucent glass that eventually could absorb a seemingly limitless palette of colors, depending upon the proportions of various oxides. When left white, it was referred to as *pâte de riz* or "alabaster glass." Among the museum's exceptional examples of this technique are a milky white opal glass vase, decorated with cutout leaves and vines painted in gold and enamel, and a gold-decorated alabaster glass bowl with opal green handles shaped like sinuous snakes, mounted on an alabaster base.

With the establishment of the Second Empire under Louis-Napoléon Bonaparte, France was to enjoy a remarkable industrial boom, typified by the 1855 Paris World's Fair. At that fair, Baccarat exhibited two huge candelabras over five meters high, each holding ninety candles,

and a chandelier with 140 lights almost five meters wide, thereby demonstrating its supremacy in crystal lighting.

The museum contains a splendid pair of 3.85-meter-high electrified candelabras that Tsar Nicholas II ordered for his palace in Saint Petersburg in 1896. However, World War I, followed by the Russian Revolution, prevented the delivery of the Tsar's candelabra—which is why they are in the museum today.

In 1907, the crystal manufacturer expanded, building a new mechanized workshop in Rambervilliers, ten miles from Baccarat, which employed women exclusively to cut perfume bottles and stoppers. Within a year, the workshop's 143 female workers were producing 4,000 bottles a day; within four years, the number rose to 5,000 a day. The largest orders

THIS ELEPHANT-SHAPED LIQUOR CABINET
IS MADE OF MOLDED
AND SCULPTED CRYSTAL AND
GILDED BRASS.
1878.
(COURTESY MUSÉE DE CRISTAL DE BACCARAT.)

were placed by the perfumers François Coty and Houbigant, as well as Guerlain, whose first crystal bottles date back to the Second Empire. Perhaps the most remarkable bottle is the one designed for Elizabeth Arden's perfume *It's You*, consisting of a white opaline hand clasping a gold perfume flacon.

The museum allots a special place for the work of its talented designer, Georges Chevalier (1894–1987). Not only did Chevalier create many novel modern designs in lighting and stemware, he also initiated the company's crystal bestiary line, examples of which are also on display.

The extraordinary partnership of industry and creativity at Baccarat that has earned international acclaim for its crystalware is movingly evoked by Ernest Tisserand in the October 1929 issue of *Art Vivant*: "In any good crystal factory, the worker's skill and personality are also important. Baccarat still has the most remarkable workers. Machines and mechanization have not in any way replaced the glass-blower's ability, virtuosity and intelligence. The hand gives the tone and the emotion."

Seeing these unique and glorious pieces of crystal in the Museum of Baccarat Crystal, it is hard to believe that each one was made from lowly sand, lead, and potash. If these beautiful, fragile objects elicit awe and delight, it is because they stand for all that is best in human perseverance, ingenuity, and artistry.

Le Musée de la Curiosité et de la Magie
The Museum of Curiosities and Magic

11, Rue Saint Paul
75004 Paris
Tel: (01) 42–72–13–26

Open Wednesday, Saturday, and
Sunday from 2:00 P.M. to 7:00 P.M.
Continuous magic show from
2:30 P.M. to 6:00 P.M.

Metro: Saint Paul or Sully-
Morland
Bus: 29

"BONJOUR!" The mechanical voice of a turbaned fortune-teller fenced in by a serpent and a large steel ball, standing inside a small sentry-box, takes the unsuspecting visitor by surprise. Constructed in the United States in the 1930s, this automaton—said to be the most photographed in the world—stood for a long time at the entrance of a movie theater on the Place Pigalle where, in exchange for a two-franc piece, a customer received his or her horoscope.

This automaton is one of 300 startling, fascinating, ludicrous, and amusing exhibits on display at the Museum of Curiosities and Magic— the only museum dedicated to the history and demonstration of magic in France. Located in a series of sixteenth-century caves in the heart of the historic Marais district (where the Marquis de Sade is said to have once held his ritual orgies), this novel museum is the brainchild of world-class magician George Proust, a collaborator with such internationally acclaimed performers as David Copperfield and Siegfried and Roy.

Open since 1993, the museum presents a panorama of art and objects dedicated to prestidigitation, including colorful graphic posters promoting popular conjurers of the last century, diverting and clever objects used for magic tricks, as well as scenic props and devices, such as the box for the woman sawed in two and the portable sedan chair that conceals a person inside until it is time for him to magically appear. The museum also boasts the very first coffin-size box used for sawing a

THIS MOTLEY FAMILY OF AUTOMATONS
AT THE MUSEUM OF CURIOSITIES AND MAGIC
REPRESENTS A VARIETY OF STYLES
AND PROFESSIONS.

woman in two, once owned by an American magician.

The biggest crowd pleaser among the museum's impressive collection of zanily costumed automatons is the soldier dressed in a Foreign Legion uniform, who greedily guzzles a clear liquid from a goblet that is replenished from an inexhaustible bottle. (A guided tour of the museum divulges the secret behind this mechanical tour-de-force.)

Then there are the gags and tricks of Proust's own devising, including a portrait of a cavalier who suddenly starts puffing smoke from a lit cigar; two long black skeletal arms that suddenly emerge from behind a painting of a hideous monster; a cupboard from which a roaring lion pops out when visitors stick in their hands; a set of peepholes which—when looked through—suddenly transform the viewer's face into that of a ghoulish old man.

The museum exhibits also include a variety of optical illusions, including a picture that resembles either a landscape by the sea or the silhouette of Napoléon Bonaparte, depending upon how you look at it; a box that seems concave but, in fact, is flat; as well as deforming mirrors that transform one's silhouette from top-model svelteness to an impressive rotundity.

Unlike most museums, where the atmosphere tends to be quietly respectful, the Museum of Curiosities

MARVO THE MYSTIC
STILL MAKES MAGIC COME ALIVE—
ONLY HERE,
INSTEAD OF CHARGING A PENNY,
HE ASKS FOR FIVE FRENCH FRANCS!

and Magic resounds with squeals of laughter, surprise, and delight. After a guided tour given in a choice of English, French, Spanish, or German, visitors are invited to enter a small theater to see a variety of tricks performed with cards, ropes, and coins. Like many magic shows, audience participation is encouraged and often turns out to be an essential part of the entertainment.

"My wish with this museum was to remove the veil from a province that is considered marginal, without getting too serious about it," Proust explains.

"The skill of a conjurer consists in producing marvels by means that are secret, but which are totally natural and explainable. Magic is such a fabulous educational tool that it should be taught in schools," he maintains. "It sharpens all the senses, develops critical thinking, and obliges a person to put himself or herself in the place of the other. Above all, it unlocks an essential insight: the hidden face of things."

The pedagogical spirit of the museum, which is exemplified by thoughtful signage and the continuous playing of an admirable video on the history of magic, demonstrates that conjury is one of the most ancient arts, dating back to the Egyptians. Ancient Greek and Roman chronicles relate that priests used their knowledge of optics, chemistry, and physics to perpetrate a variety of hoaxes. The scientist and inventor, Hero of Alexandria (also known as Heron), wrote of bottomless vases and miraculous fountains that dispensed an inexhaustible supply of wine or water. The museum displays an architectural blueprint demonstrating the manner in which a mechanism was triggered that opened a temple's door when its altar was set on fire. "The priest was a religious figure,

THIS BRONZE BUST
IS OF ROBERT HOUDIN,
FRANCE'S MOST FAMOUS MAGICIAN.
NEXT TO IT IS
A FIRST EDITION OF HIS MAJOR WORK,
ENTITLED
CONFIDENCES ET RÉVÉLATIONS
(CONFIDENCES AND REVELATIONS),
AND THE TYPES OF PROPS
THAT HE ONCE USED IN HIS
PERFORMANCES.

a scientist and a conjurer—he used illusions to impress and exert power over the gullible," Proust notes.

Still, magic wasn't of interest only to priests. Plautus (254 B.C.–184 B.C.), the Roman comic poet and playwright, who inspired both Shakespeare and Molière, writes of magic as a theatrical art and discusses the conjurers of his time. Seneca (3 B.C.–A.D. 65), the Stoic philosopher, also described a variety of popular tricks, such as those performed with balls and goblets.

However, by the Middle Ages, even as minstrels and fools continued to entertain the royal courts with conjury, magicians were suspected of

THE OLDEST EXTANT PROP USED
FOR SAWING A PERSON IN TWO
WAS ONCE OWNED
BY THE AMERICAN MAGICIAN
HENRY THURSTON.

important to remember that until a few hundred years ago, most scientific phenomena were regarded as magical," notes Proust.

The museum pays special homage to Robert Houdin (1805–1870), regarded as the father of modern magic or "white magic," displaying his bronze bust in a vitrine. Beside his bust is a first edition of his major work, *Confidences et Révélations, Comment On Devient Sorcier (Confidences and Revelations, How One Becomes a Magician)*. This celebrated watchmaker, inventor of optical instruments, as well as an early version of the incandescent lamp (which Thomas Edison would later perfect), became the first magician to wear evening clothes and bring glamour and refinement to a much maligned art. At his *Théâtre de la Magie* (Magic Theater), which he opened in 1848 on the Boulevard des Italiens in Paris, he demonstrated such popular tricks as the inexhaustible bottle and the cane that could be suspended in mid-air. This same theater would later be run by the pioneering film-maker Georges Méliès, who was himself a magician.

Houdin was so widely respected and admired that the famed American magician Eric Weiss (1887–1924) changed his name to Harry Houdini, in homage to the Frenchman. Later however, after he was snubbed by Houdin's widow during a tour abroad, he took his revenge by trying to destroy the magician's reputation with a book entitled *The Unmasking of Robert Houdin*.

While the museum's vitrines display many intriguing props and tools that have figured in magic shows for the past century or so, little is revealed about how they work. "Like all magicians we have sworn a vow to secrecy," explains Proust. "Only those who belong to the Club of Magicians

heresy and Devil worship. Hence, the emergence of the term "black magic." In 1066, the Lex Salica condemned all magic entertainments; those who persisted in conjury risked being burned at the stake. According to the museum's video, it was only during the Renaissance that conjurers made their reappearance at country fairs. The first work dedicated to prestidigitation, by Jean Prévost, was published in 1584. In it were descriptions of tricks with goblets, fruits and ropes, under the title *First Part of Subtle and Delightful Inventions*.

Slowly, magic began to reappear at court. The nobility, and later the wealthy bourgeoisie, built *cabinets de physique* (offices dedicated to the study of physics) in their homes, where they held séances and demonstrated inventions for the amusement and pleasure of their guests. "It's

in Paris are privy to how these tricks work." For those eager to learn more about the ins and outs of "white magic," the museum offers a two-year program where novices are taught the basics, including cartomancy.

After an afternoon at this delightfully perplexing museum, it is easy to see why the fascination of magic has cast its spell over such varied personalities as Wolfgang von Goethe, Alfred de Musset, Louis Pasteur, Auguste Lumière, Sacha Guitry, Orson Welles, and the Duke of Windsor.

"More than anything else, magic is the art of communication. You have to insinuate yourself into the mind of the other person, while you are doing a trick," notes Proust. "Because it's so visual, people can understand it, even without language. Perhaps that's why this museum attracts people from all over the world."

THESE STAGE PROPS WERE ONCE USED
TO MAKE PEOPLE APPEAR
AND DISAPPEAR.

Le Musée National Eugène Delacroix
The Eugène Delacroix Museum

6, Rue de Furstenberg
75006 Paris
Tel: (01) 43-54-04-87

Open every day except Tuesday
from 9:45 A.M. to 12:30 P.M.
and from 2:00 P.M. to 5:15 P.M.

Metro: Saint Germain-des-Prés
Bus: 48, 63, 86, 87, 96

A VIEW OF THE GARDEN
AND THE ATELIER,
WHICH WERE BUILT
ACCORDING TO
THE ARTIST'S STRICT
SPECIFICATIONS.

O N DECEMBER 29, 1857, Eugène Delacroix (1798–1863) moved into a lovely apartment in the former commons of the Abbey of Saint-Germain-des-Prés at 6 Rue de Furstenberg on the Left Bank. Nothing could have been more practical or necessary: seriously ill with tubercular laryngitis, he had chosen this quiet retreat within a courtyard in order to be close to the Saint-Sulpice Church, where he was completing his final public commission — three frescoes inside the Saintes-Anges Chapel.

Thanks to his friend, Ernest Haro, who sold him his paints, he had found this calm and airy lodging, only minutes away on foot from the church. The only thing missing was an atelier. With great dispatch, Delacroix commissioned the owner of the late-eighteenth-century dwelling to build him a spacious studio according to his specifications in the delightful tree-lined garden. A staircase made of steel was joined to the apartment, thus facilitating access to the studio.

Today, visitors can experience the same quiet serenity and peacefulness at the Eugène Delacroix Museum, located in the painter's former studio and apartment. Although there is a discreet plaque on the Place de Furstenberg, just outside the archway leading to the museum, many people walk right past it, never suspecting the untold riches within. That the museum exists at all, is due largely to the concerted efforts of two painters, Maurice Denis and Paul Signac. By founding the Société des Amis d'Eugène Delacroix in 1929, these two artists—together with a number of other Delacroix aficionados—were able to save the painter's only extant home and studio from being destroyed and turned into a parking garage.

While most of Delacroix's greatest works are in the Louvre and in other collections around the world, this charming museum harbors many smaller works that provide a sort of short-form biography of his achievements as one of the leading painters of the Romantic school. This collection includes such religious paintings as *La Descente au Tombeau (The Descent into the Tomb)* and *La Montée au Calvaire (The Ascent to Calvary)* as well as the *Autoportrait en Hamlet (Self-Portrait as Hamlet)* and *Turc Assis (Seated Turk)*. The museum's most important work is the artist's second version of *L'Enlèvement de Rebecca (The Kidnapping of Rebecca)*, the other being in the Louvre. Moreover, since the artist's home was declared a national museum in 1954, it has also been the site of many temporary exhibitions focusing on different aspects of this prolific painter's work.

The walls of Delacroix's airy, light-filled studio are lined with twenty-two watercolor copies of the frescoes that the artist painted on the ceiling of the library in the Chamber of Deputies. These copies were executed by the painter René Piot, when he restored the frescoes from 1928 to 1930.

It is also in this atelier that one can see the wooden easel, two oak painting tables, and the palette that belonged to the painter. It was here that Delacroix conceived the seven paintings he submitted to the Salon of 1859 (his last). Despite several relapses, he managed to paint such major works as *La Montée au Calvaire (The Ascent to Calvary)*, *La Descente au Tombeau (The Descent into the Tomb)*, and *Hamlet et Horatio au Cimetière (Hamlet and Horatio at the Cemetery)*.

THE DELACROIX STUDIO: HIS PAINTBOX AND EASEL, UPON WHICH RESTS A STUNNING FULL-LENGTH MALE NUDE.

During this period he wrote to his most loyal confidante, George Sand: "For the past four months I am doing a job that has restored the health I thought I had lost; I get up in the morning, I run to work, I return as late as I can, and I start over the next day. . . . Nothing seduces me more than painting; and here on top of everything it has given me the health of a thirty-year-old, [Delacroix was sixty-three]; my only thought is for her, it's only for her that I rack my brains, that is I think I throw myself into my work as Newton did in his famous quest of gravitation. . . ."

Still, his main achievement was the work done in "his chapel," which he worked on steadily from May 1859 until July 1861. According to the artist and restorer René Piot, it was in this very atelier that Delacroix "made his final sketches and deliberated over his final musings regarding his Saint-Sulpice masterpiece. The austere lyricism of the Saintes-Anges Chapel is the fruit of the old master's reveries under the trees of this garden, in this silent retreat."

Out of that rhapsodic creative state emerged three frescoes: *L'Archange Saint Michel Terrassant le Démon* (*The Archangel Michael Defeating the Devil*) on the ceiling; *Héliodore Chassé du Temple* (*Héliodore Chased from the Temple*) on the right wall, and *La Lutte de Jacob avec l'Ange* (*The Struggle of Jacob with the Angel*) on the left.

Although the Saint-Sulpice frescoes are in dire need of cleaning and restoration (a project now underway), they were greatly praised by such critics as Théophile Gautier and Charles Baudelaire, among others.

At his side through all these travails was his faithful servant and governess, Jenny Le Guillou (1801–1869), whose stern yet compassionate portrait hangs in Delacroix's handsomely restored bedroom over the marble fireplace mantel. Little remains of its original furnishings, apart from the artist's narrow bed covered in dark green velvet, a chair, and an elaborately carved end table. The windows in this room, like all the others, have been purposefully hung with heavy double curtains made of garnet-colored velvet, similar to those chosen by the painter when he lived here.

Seeing the painter's narrow bed, one feels overwhelmed by a feeling of poignancy, knowing that this is where he lay, unable to work or move, during the last few months of his life.

A week after his death, Le Guillou wrote in a letter to Madame Bahut, one of Delacroix's former students: "My poor dear master was sick for the past three months; the illness began as a cold as always, and his poor chest got infected; all this time I nursed him without leaving him for a single instant; he remained calm and serene until the final hour, recognizing me, pressing my hands without being able to speak until he gave his last breath like a child."

Delacroix never forgot the unflagging care and loyalty of this simple Breton peasant woman, whom he would invite to accompany him on his visits to the Louvre. In his will, the painter made her his principal beneficiary, leaving her 50,000 francs, as well as any furniture she might want from his apartment.

Thanks to inventory records set down shortly after the artist's death, curator Arlette Sérullaz was able to assemble detailed information concerning the exact furniture that was in the apartment. Judging by the description of the furnishings, now indicated on special wall panels in each room, the apartment during Delacroix's time was overflowing with bric-à-brac and heavy but comfortable Louis-Philippe furniture.

Mindful of the fact that this museum was previously a private home, Sérullaz has chosen to maintain its intimate nature to the greatest extent possible. At the same time, she realizes that the paucity of personal effects left by the artist makes such a task quite daunting. "Since it was out of the question to reconstruct the apartment as it was when Delacroix lived here, I tried to evoke the atmosphere of an apartment. Each room has double curtains to remind the visitor that Delacroix was constantly feeling chilled and was very vulnerable to any drafts. He was practically suffocating during the final months of his life."

According to Sérullaz, in his weakened state, Delacroix did very little entertaining, a marked contrast with the days when he played host to such luminaries as George Sand, Frédéric Chopin, Charles Baudelaire, and Henri Beyle (Stendahl). The most frequent visitor to Rue de Furstenberg was Pierre Andrieu, his student and collaborator on those frescoes that Delacroix executed for the Chamber of Deputies.

Anyone in search of extensive personal memorabilia and mementoes of Delacroix's life will not find them in this museum. Yet, Sérullaz believes a visit to the Eugène Delacroix Museum helps people to view this Romantic genius within the context of his own time. "I think it's important that people don't have too abstract an idea of this painter," she adds. "I would like them to see how he lived." Judging by the continuous flow of mail from visitors, it is obvious that this singular museum has succeeded in establishing a bond between current admirers and its former occupant. Perhaps that is why a letter recently delivered was addressed to "M. Eugène Delacroix, 6, Rue de Furstenberg," intimating that this unparalleled artist is still very much in residence.

IN HIS SUN-DRENCHED STUDIO
ARE MEMENTOES
DELACROIX BROUGHT BACK FROM
HIS TRIP TO MOROCCO,
INCLUDING A PAINTED CHEST,
SABERS, AND
STRING INSTRUMENTS.

Le Musée Départemental Maurice Denis
— Le "Prieuré"

The Maurice Denis Museum — The "Priory"

2 bis, Rue Maurice Denis
78100 Saint-Germain-en-Laye
Tel: (01) 39-73-77-87

**Open Wednesday through Friday
from 10:00 A.M. to 5:30 P.M.;
Saturday, Sunday, and holidays
from 10:00 A.M. to 6:30 P.M.**

Access:

- **By Metro/R.E.R.: Take Line A
from Châtelet, direction Saint-
Germain-en-Laye, get off at the
stop Saint-Germain-en-Laye, take
Bus 158 next to the Château de
Saint-Germain-en-Laye, get off at
Rue Schnapper, and turn right to
the Rue Maurice Denis.**

- **By car: Take the Autoroute A13
from the Porte d'Auteuil, until the
second exit, direction Saint-
Germain-en-Laye, take the
Nationale 184, which turns into
Nationale 13, until the exit Saint-
Germain-en-Laye, Hôpital-Sous-
Préfecture, and follow the signs
"Musée du Prieuré" until you
reach the Rue du Fourqueux, turn
right until you reach the Maurice
Denis Museum.**

IN 1678, the Marquise de
Montespan (1640–1707), the mistress of King Louis XIV, with whom
she had eight children, acquired a
secluded property of two-and-a-half
acres in Saint-Germain-en-Laye for
17,000 pounds, with the intention of
building a hospital to serve the poor.
According to records from this
period, the aims of the hospital were
not only charitable; the establishment
of this institution was also intended as
a preventive measure to keep the des-
titute from begging from the wealthy.

Inaugurated in 1681 as a General
Royal Hospital by one of the
Marquise's sons, this majestic two-
story edifice extended fifty-four
meters in length and included a
chapel, commons, and administrative
quarters, as well as basement cells for
the more unruly patients. After the
hospital closed in 1803, the building
passed through a number of different
hands. In 1875, the Jesuits acquired
the estate and used it as a religious
retreat until 1905, when the French
Republic passed a law separating
Church and State.

The French painter Maurice Denis
(1870–1943), who had grown up in
Saint-Germain-en-Laye, had always
wished to live in this stately and
imposing building—a dream he was
finally able to realize in 1913. The
property's gardens, woods, and
spartan chapel appealed to the solitary
artist, who was a man of immense
religious fervor and restraint.
Renaming the house and wooded
grounds the "Priory," after the name
of the street outside its walls, Denis

worked and lived on the estate for the next thirty years, surrounded by his large family of six children and two step-children, and his many friends, who numbered among them the leading artists and intellectuals of the day.

Today, visitors to Saint-Germain-en-Laye can discover the spellbinding property that so delighted the artist and his notable friends. Following the bequest of Maurice Denis's paintings to the department of the Yvelines by the artist's heirs, the department acquired the "Priory" in 1976 and transformed it into the Maurice Denis Museum, which opened in 1980.

"Denis, who was a mystic, was deeply affected by the mystery this estate inspired: the chapel which he decorated and the winding paths of the park and isolated nooks, conceived by the Jesuits for reflection and contemplation, were favorable to the esoteric and symbolic inspiration of this great artist," observes Agnès Dellanoy, the museum's curator.

At the "Priory," Denis developed his ideas as the principal theoretician of the "Nabis." It was he who came up with the famous statement, "One should remember that a painting, before being a battlefield, a naked woman or an incident, is essentially a flat surface covered with colors in a certain orderly arrangement."

The term "Nabi" comes from the word *nabi*, which means "prophet" in Hebrew and Arabic. This art movement was initiated in October 1888 by Paul Sérusier, who—under the direction of Paul Gauguin—painted *Le Paysage au Bois d'Amour (Landscape in the Woods of Love)*, a work that would become the group's talisman. It was after this critical meeting with Gauguin that Sérusier came to feel that he had (as his mentor had assured him), "the right to dare everything."

A VIEW OF THE
MAURICE DENIS MUSEUM,
A FORMER SEVENTEENTH-CENTURY HOSPICE
BUILT FOR THE MARQUISE DE MONTESPAN,
THE MISTRESS OF LOUIS XIV.

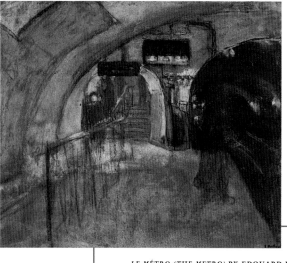

In their rebellion against academic art, the Nabis—who eventually included such artists as Edouard Vuillard, Pierre Bonnard, Maurice Denis, Georges Desvallières, Henri-Gabriel Ibels, Paul Ranson, Georges Lacombe, Jozsef Rippl-Ronai, and Francesco-Mogens Ballin—produced posters, theater sets, book illustrations, furniture, tapestries, stained-glass windows, and decorated fans, as well as paintings and sculpture.

"The Nabis were a group of artists whose idea of painting was to take objective reality as a point of departure and use it to reveal the soul," notes Claire Denis, the painter's grand-daughter, who has played a pivotal role in the museum's creation. "Their objective was to paint mystery and reveal the unspoken. At the same time, inspired by Gauguin, they wanted to concentrate on a single sensation and feeling, and emphasize it as much as possible."

Adds Dellanoy: "The Nabis period constituted an important turning point in art, a sort of intense concentration of energy as well as a necessary progression. It was the beginning of a period that would lead to the explosion of Fauvism, as well as Expressionism and Abstract art in the early years of this century."

With a nearly forty-year hiatus between the death of Denis and the opening of the museum, it is understandable that the building's interior has been vastly altered since the artist was in residence. Still, the building's austere but handsome seventeenth-century stone archways, wood-beamed ceilings, and stately staircase have been retained, and serve to enhance the artwork on display.

On the ground floor, five spacious, light-filled rooms are allotted to Denis's paintings, murals, graphics, set designs, furniture, stained-glass windows, and mosaics; on the second floor, six rooms are dedicated to works by other Nabis, many of whom collaborated closely with Denis. The third floor, once the building's attic, is reserved for temporary exhibitions of work held in the reserves.

Although the museum's interior is spacious, the breadth of the collection is such that even the galleries and stairwells contain paintings, posters, and furnishings by Symbolists, post-Impressionists, and artists from the Pont-Aven school—all of whom had close ties to Denis.

When the artist was commissioned to execute the vast frescoes intended for the ceiling of the Theater of the Champs-Elysées, he found the studio he was using in the former hospital to be too small. He therefore asked Auguste Perret (the theater's architect) to design a studio in the "Priory's" garden. Today, this restored atelier is used to display Denis's various sketches, and drafts of his large religious and secular projects.

Nowhere is the religious zeal and artistry of Denis more present than in the Saint-Louis chapel, which he restored once he and his family had moved into the "Priory." With the exception of the frescoes of the *Beatitudes,* which were painted by his students in 1928, the artist managed to redecorate the whole church with frescoes representing the Stations of the Cross, as well as designing its stained-glass windows, altar, candelabra, and altar sculptures. For those art lovers who know and appreciate the work of Denis, this museum presents many of his principal works, including the enchanting ceiling fresco *L'Echelle dans le Feuillage (The Ladder Within the Foliage), Madame Ranson au Chat (Madame Ranson and Her Cat),* and *Le Dessert au Jardin (Dessert in the Garden),* as well as numerous drawings and preparatory sketches for religious and civil buildings.

In addition to doing a laudable job of presenting the full range of Denis's multifaceted oeuvre —the museum also boasts a fine collection of work by the artist's contemporaries. Among the notable masters exhibited in the collection are Emile Bernard, Pierre Bonnard, Paul Gauguin, Paul Sérusier, James Ensor, Hector Guimard, Alfred Jarry, Alphonse Mucha, Pierre Puvis de Chavannes, Théo van Rysselberghe, and Claude-Emile Schuffenecker.

The collection also contains the unexpected, including an intriguing painting by Vuillard entitled *Le Métro (The Metro)*, a mysterious figurative work by Piet Mondrian, *Femmes dans un Bois (Women in a Woodland)*, as well as a splendid Pointillist full-

TOTEM BY
JULES PARESSANT;
BRONZE SCULPTURE IN THE
REAR BY HADJU.

AN ENCHANTING TRELLISED
WHITE ROSE GARDEN
IS ONE OF THE LOVELY FEATURES OF
THE PROPERTY AT THE
MAURICE DENIS MUSEUM.
(COPYRIGHT MUSÉE MAURICE DENIS.)

length portrait by Théo van Rysselberghe, *Portrait d'Alice Sethe*.

If the weather is fine, one shouldn't miss a delightful walk along the terraced path lined with a row of splendid linden trees next to the "Priory," reminiscent of a landscape in Tuscany. Strolling down the winding lanes that once so captivated Denis and his friends, visitors will come upon a delightful rose garden, an orchard, a vegetable and a medicinal garden.

In such an enchanting environment, it is easy to understand why Maurice Denis was captivated by these peaceful surroundings. In his journal, Denis wrote: "I am dreaming of a purified brotherhood of committed artists who would be lovers of beauty and the good, and who, both in their works and their lives, would express this indefinable trait which can only be called 'Nabi'." Those who visit the "Priory" will happily find that its collections are a tribute to this artist's fervent hope and lifelong commitment.

Le Musée de l'Eventail

The Fan Museum

2, Boulevard Strasbourg
75010 Paris
Tel: (01) 42–08–90–20

**Open Tuesday afternoon from
2:00 P.M. to 5:00 P.M. Group visits
available with advance reservations.**

Metro: Strasbourg-Saint-Denis
Bus: 39, 47

DURING THE Belle Epoque, elegant women of all ages took special delight in a trip to Lepault et Deberghe, one of the most sought-after fan-makers in Paris, which opened an elegant showroom in 1893 not far from the Place de la République. Alone or in the company of a wealthy husband or lover, they would come to admire the enticing displays of custom-made fans composed of the most splendid and exotic materials from all over the world. Only the finest and rarest components were used: hand-painted silk, satin, swan skin, chromolithographed paper, Chantilly lace, tulle, organza, and paillettes—any one or combinations of which were ingeniously mounted to frames made of precious woods, mother-of-pearl, ivory, and horn, often inlaid with gold and precious jewels.

Fans were the quintessential accessory for the woman of fashion whether she was attending the opera, the races, the theater, or paying a social call. They were often given as gifts to commemorate the most important occasions, particularly births, coming-out balls, engagements, and marriages. Even when in mourning, a woman would carry a proper fan. It would take the guns and flames of World War I and the advent of the flapper and the hip flask to put an end to the widespread usage of fans among the upper classes.

Yet, thanks to curator and collector Anne Hoguet, France's only known surviving fan-maker, visitors can rediscover this all but vanished art at the Fan Museum, which she opened in 1993 in the very same showroom where Lepault et Deberghe once carried on a thriving business.

The spacious atelier's interior is much enlivened by a rotating display of eighteenth-, nineteenth-, and twentieth-century silk, paper, beaded, ivory, and feather fans, many of which are carefully preserved and mounted in glass display cases. Time seems to have stood still in this showroom, which still retains its period Henry II Renaissance decor, ornately carved chimneypiece, and walnut cabinets where the fans are still stored. The walls are covered with the original royal blue silk brocade embroidered with gold fleurs-de-lys, and its palatial coffered ceiling is set off by three chandeliers from the same era. Such a regal backdrop seems entirely fitting for an accessory which only the nobility was allowed to carry until the French Revolution.

A tour of this intimate two-room museum offers not only a feast for the eye, but a well-documented history of fan-making, with displays showing the tools of the trade, the raw materials that went into making a fan, as well as engravings of many of the painstaking and time-consuming tasks associated with this all but forgotten vocation. (Since Hoguet and her colleagues spend a portion of their time restoring antique fans and creating special editions for French couturiers, visitors may have the rare opportunity of seeing an actual fan being assembled and decorated.)

The museum's finest examples of eighteenth-and nineteenth-century fans have exquisite filigree mounts and finely painted fan leaves featuring episodes from classical mythology, history, and religion, as well as romantic and bucolic scenes. The minute details of each fan help explain why these small-scale works of art often took as long as eighteen months to complete and cost as much

as a new car would today. According to Hoguet a woman at court might own as many as fifteen of these extravagant accessories.

The first fans, made of peacock feathers, papyrus, and palm-fronds, were developed simultaneously and independently about five thousand years ago in Egypt and China. The Chinese transformed fans into an art, whereas the Egyptians used them as a mark of class distinction. It seems that the French saw them as both.

In Egypt slaves would wave huge fans of palm fronds and papyrus to cool their wealthy masters; in China, fans varied in both design and decoration. Besides the peacock feather fan, the Chinese developed the "screen" fan, made of silk fabric stretched over a bamboo frame and mounted on a lacquered handle. In the sixth century A.D., they introduced the screen fan to the Japanese, who, in turn, conceived an ingenious modification: the folding fan. The Japanese folding fan consisted of a solid silk cloth attached to a series of sticks that collapsed one on top of the other.

In the tenth century, the Japanese introduced the folding fan to China. At that point, not to be outdone, the Chinese made a clever modification: dispensing with the solid silk cloth stretched over separate sticks, they substituted a series of "blades" in bamboo or ivory. These thin blades, threaded together at their tops by a ribbon, actually constituted the fan, which was also collapsible. The "blade" fan, or *brisé* as it came to be called, is the most sought-after fan, and the museum has some stunning examples in mother-of-pearl and tortoiseshell, both painted and unpainted.

Beginning in the fifteenth century, European merchants, notably Portuguese traders, imported a variety of decorative Chinese and Japanese

TWO EXAMPLES OF FRENCH
EIGHTEENTH-CENTURY *BRISÉ* FANS FEATURING
BUCOLIC AND MYTHOLOGICAL SCENES.
THESE FANS, WHICH TOOK
AS LONG AS EIGHTEEN MONTHS TO MAKE
AND WHICH COST AS MUCH AS A CAR WOULD TODAY,
WERE CARRIED ONLY BY THE QUEEN
AND HER COURT
UNTIL THE FRENCH REVOLUTION.

fans to Europe, many of them featuring handles inlaid with precious stones, and ornamented with golden or silver chains that could be suspended from a lady's belt. Hoguet believes that Italian merchants at the court of Catherine de' Medicis first imported these dazzling accessories to France. "It was from that time that we can date the manufacturing of fans in France," she notes. (It's an interesting coincidence that the same Henry II who inspired the showroom's decor was also husband to Catherine de' Medicis.)

The fashion for carrying fans was promoted even more extensively during the reign of Louis XIII. His spouse, Anne of Austria, brought the Spanish taste for fans with her and made it an integral part of the toilette of her ladies-in-waiting. In fact, it was the Spanish who transformed the fan into a much-prized instrument of courtship, used partly to maintain an air of secrecy and discretion. For instance, a woman who tucked her fan under her chin indicated her love to a suitor. If she held the edge of her fan with her hand, it meant the contrary.

It wasn't long before fan-making became a major industry in Paris and its outskirts; by 1678 Louis XIV had established a fan-making guild. In the eighteenth century the first major fan-making ateliers were opened at Sainte-Geneviève in the Oise region, and eventually spread to the nearby townships of Noailles, Andeville, and Méru. It was in Sainte-Geneviève that Hoguet's forebear, Joseph Hoguet

Duroyaume, created his atelier for fan frames. The fan leaf was decorated and mounted separately in Paris.

Up until World War I, there were as many as sixty fan-makers employing an estimated 1,200 workers, most of them in the vicinity of this former showroom. "As many as twenty people worked on a single fan," says Hoguet, "including those in the feather and paper trade, as well as leather workers, gilders, painters, lacemakers and embroiderers."

France made fans not only for Spain, but for England and Holland, which exported them as far as the Baltic, as well as to North and South America. After World War I, fan-making was basically limited to promotional or theatrical vehicles: the museum's collection includes 150 fans from the 1920s and 1930s advertising such department stores as Le Bon Marché and La Samaritaine, as well as a variety of alcoholic beverages, cafés, and restaurants.

Although the era of hand-painted and ostrich feather fans is long-gone (the exception being the fans still used in floor shows, such as those at the Lido and the Folies-Bergère), the museum does have a limited collection of unique fans created in the 1970s and 1980s for such noted designers as Karl Lagerfeld, Nina Ricci, Jean-Louis Scherrer, Christian Lacroix, and Isabel Canovas. These fans were used mainly as accessories for the haute couture collections.

Today, the Fan Museum's collection numbers close to 800 French fans, which are sometimes augmented by loans for temporary exhibitions. Like all passionate collectors, Hoguet has her favorites. "I prefer the fans made in the nineteenth century, because they are the most romantic, even if they aren't necessarily the finest," she says. Sentimentalists are likely to be captivated by the museum's extensive collection of hand-painted fans, which are paeans to feminine beauty, youth, and love's gallantries.

Why does Hoguet think fans continue to exert their fascination? "More than anything else, fans are objects of seduction and mystery," she explains. "A woman holding a fan is much more alluring than one holding a cigarette." After a visit to this charming, original museum, one would find it difficult to disagree.

Le Musée Maillol — Fondation Dina Vierny

The Maillol Museum — The Dina Vierny Foundation

59–61, Rue de Grenelle
75007 Paris
Tel: (01) 42–22–59–58

**Open Wednesday through Monday
11:00 A.M. to 6:00 P.M.**

Metro: Rue du Bac
Bus: 68, 69, 83, 84

ARISTIDE MAILLOL,
LA BAIGNEUSE DRAPÉE OU LA SEINE
(THE DRAPED BATHER OR THE SEINE)
1921.
(©1996 ARTISTS RIGHTS SOCIETY,
ARS, N.Y./SPADEM, PARIS.)

ARISTIDE MAILLOL (1861–1944), who fought against the narrow observance of academic conventions all his life, never aspired to belong to the artistic establishment. Despite universal acclaim of his works, he was never recognized as an official sculptor in France. It would take the passion and persistent efforts of a single woman, Maillol's former muse and model, Dina Vierny, to inaugurate in January 1995 the only museum dedicated to preserving and exhibiting the complete range of this artist's work, and to present it in the company of many works by his peers: Pierre Bonnard, Paul Gauguin, Henri Matisse, Odilon Redon, Auguste Rodin, and Raoul Dufy.

Vierny, who has run a very successful gallery in Paris since the end of World War II, inherited Maillol's estate after the death of his son, Lucien. The works on display in this museum were either given to her or were acquired through her gallery. Sales of Maillol's work to museums, galleries, and private collectors eventually made it possible to finance an institution bearing the sculptor's name. This pristine and original museum represents the culmination of fifteen years of tireless work, drive, and ingenuity.

Walking through the stunning ground-floor exhibition area, with its smoothly polished marble floors, rough stone walls made with boulders from Burgundy, and exposed-beam ceiling—now home to some of Maillol's most monumental sculptures —it is difficult to conceive that this four-story museum once had such diverse tenants as a fishmonger, a

ROUGH BURGUNDIAN STONE AND SMOOTH MARBLE FLOORS
WERE CHOSEN FOR THE LOBBY OF THE MAILLOL MUSEUM, A FITTING BACKDROP
FOR THE SCULPTOR'S WORK SHOWN HERE.
(©1996 ARTISTS RIGHTS SOCIETY, ARS, N.Y./SPADEM, PARIS.)

photo agency, and a pharmaceutical laboratory, as well as one of the city's most famous jazz clubs, "Le Cabaret des Quatre Saisons."

"This museum had to be created," Vierny asserts. "Maillol is the greatest French sculptor after Rodin. His sculpture is very special—very inward, silent, sensual, and knowing. When people visit here, they come away happy."

Vierny first met Maillol as a fifteen-year-old teenager in Paris. After the architect of the Musée de l'Art Moderne confided to Maillol that he knew of a young woman who—strangely enough—resembled Maillol's work, the sculptor wrote her: "Mademoiselle, it appears that you resemble a Maillol and a Renoir; I will be happy if it's a Renoir." Shortly afterward, the precocious Dina, who was familiar with the Surrealists and a friend of André Breton, met Maillol one Sunday in his atelier at Marly-le-Roi. From that day onward began a collaboration between artist and model that would last ten years, until Maillol's death at the age of eighty-three.

"When I met him in 1934, he was seventy-three years old and had stopped making sculpture," Vierny recalls. "He told me that after seeing me I sparked his desire to return to work.

"He was surprised that I understood his work and could help him to fulfill it," she adds. "In a way, I was able to be the substance of his thought."

About Maillol, she recalls: "He was a man filled with kindness. Until the end, he remained generous and funny." Vierny had reason to appreciate these qualities. When she was captured by the Nazis as a young girl involved with the French Resistance, it was Maillol who negotiated her release, through the Third Reich's official sculptor, Arno Brecker, who admired and supported the French sculptor's work.

Vierny not only inspired such major sculptures as *La Montagne*, 1937 *(The Mountain)*, *L'Air*, 1938 *(The Air)*, and *La Rivière*, 1941 *(The River)*, as well as Maillol's final unfinished work *l'Harmonie*, 1942–43 *(Harmony)*, but beautiful sensuous paintings, pastels, and drawings as well.

Maillol, however, was not the only artist who used her as a model. In May 1941, after Matisse had undergone a serious operation that had rendered him practically immobile, Maillol sent Dina to him with this note of encouragement: "I am lending you the inspiration for my work, you will render her in a single line." Judging by the lively linear drawings of the nude Dina, all of which Matisse executed in 1941 (now on display in the museum), Maillol's prediction was correct. Vierny remembers her sessions with Matisse as candid and delightful. "His hand traced the form of my body with India ink: he drew me as an odalisque of 1941 wearing raffia sandals, because there was nothing else we could find. 'Because you resemble the Olympia of Manet, I would like to paint you as the Olympia of Matisse,' he told me."

Unfortunately, Matisse was never able to fulfill this vision, being forced to "share" Dina with the painter Pierre Bonnard, who had already started on a large nude of the young woman. This beautiful, richly colored painting, *Nu sombre*, 1941–44, *(Dark Nude)*, also hangs in the museum.

It is apparent that Vierny had a fundamental influence upon Maillol's work during the final decade of his life. Her lifelong commitment to Maillol now makes it possible for

THIS GALLERY SHOWS
MAILLOL'S EARLY VIRTUOSITY AS A PAINTER
BEFORE HE TURNED TO SCULPTURE;
THE LARGE CANVAS, *SEATED WOMAN WITH A PARASOL*,
WAS PAINTED IN 1895.

connoisseurs and amateurs alike to see and appreciate both the range and the specific achievements of this revolutionary artist, who was to herald the work of Brancusi and the Cubist sculptors.

The museum's comprehensive collection of sculptures in wood, clay, plaster, bronze, and marble reveals Maillol's unending quest for a singularity of line and simplicity of form that would cause Rodin to say of him: "What is admirable in Maillol, what I could say is eternal, is the purity, the clarity, the lucidity of his craft and his thought."

The museum's rich collection demonstrates that Maillol's lengthy artistic career united all disciplines, including painting, drawing, ceramics, wood carving—even tapestry-making. Each of the works on display shows the artist's surprising mastery of whichever medium he undertook to explore: nowhere is this more evident than in his marvelous tapestry *Le Jardin Enchanté*, 1895 *(The Enchanted Garden)*, inspired by the colors and technique of the medieval tapestries of *La Dame à la Licorne (The Lady with the Unicorn)* in the Cluny Museum.

While more than half of this unique museum is dedicated to the works of Maillol and his contemporaries, it also pays homage to other major artistic currents of the century, particularly Surrealism, Abstract Painting, and French Primitivism.

Ample wall space has been set aside to show India ink drawings, watercolors, and oils by Wassily Kandinsky (1886–1944), drawings, gouaches, and mixed-media pieces by Jean Pougny (1892–1956), as well as abstract works by Serge Poliakoff (1900–1969). An early advocate of French Primitivism—when many

THE LOBBY OF THE MUSÉE MAILLOL.
L'ACTION ENCHAÎNÉE (CHAINED ACTION) IN THE FOREGROUND; *LA DOULEUR (SORROW)*, TO THE RIGHT; *L'ÂGE D'AIRAIN (THE BRONZE AGE)* BY AUGUSTE RODIN IN THE BACKGROUND.
(©1996 ARTISTS RIGHTS SOCIETY, ARS, N.Y./SPADEM, PARIS.)

other critics were denigrating the merits of this movement—Vierny has set aside extensive display space for such painters as Le Douanier Rousseau (1844–1910), Louis Vivin (1861–1936), André Bauchant (1873–1958), Camille Bambois (1883–1966), and René Rimbert (1896–1991). Many of these works once belonged to critic and collector Wilhelm Uhde, the first major art reviewer to champion the importance of these artists.

Vierny's admiration for the Surrealists is also evident in two rooms that are dedicated to the work of the Duchamp brothers: the ready-mades of Marcel Duchamp, the work of Raymond Duchamp-Villon, and the paintings of Jacques Villon. While the paintings and sculptures are all originals, the conceptual works by Duchamp are duplicates he made in 1964 of famous earlier works, including *In Advance of the Broken Arm*,

1915 (a snow-shovel), *Fontaine*, 1917 (a urinal in white porcelain) and *Why not Sneeze Rose Sélavy*, 1921 (a square white metal birdcage filled with sugar cubes made of marble).

Vierny's quest for new talent took her behind the Iron Curtain to what was then the Soviet Union, between 1969 and 1974. "I was curious to see how one could paint under conditions of captivity," she explains. "What struck me more than anything else is that these artists were able to work in total obscurity, as if they had been shut up in a windowless room."

The works of three conceptual artists that Vierny managed to bring to the West, are prominently displayed in the museum: the painters Eric Boulatov (born 1938), Vladimir Yankelevski (born 1928), and Ilya Kabakov (born 1933), regarded as one of the most important artists of his generation. His installation, *The Communal Kitchen*, 1993, which combines painting, writing, as well as ordinary kitchen implements, including pots, pans, and dishtowels which the artist has chosen to hang from the ceiling and the walls, is both bizarre and unsettling—a startling metaphor for the banal quotidian endured by millions of Soviet citizens.

Olivier Lorquin, the museum's co-director, hopes that visitors will come to realize that this unique institution illustrates the wide-ranging appreciation of a collector and gallery owner who has never shied away from being in the forefront of twentieth-century art movements, whatever these might be. "This museum represents the aesthetic development of an art lover," he says. "It is the work of a woman who has always defended a certain perception of what is art. She was among the first to see what others would come to see only much later. Now, she wants to share that vision with the world."

LA MÉDITERRANÉE (THE MEDITERRANEAN)
(SECOND STATE). 1902–05.
(©1996 ARTISTS RIGHTS SOCIETY,
ARS, N.Y./SPADEM, PARIS.)

THIS MAGNIFICENT TORSO
BY RODIN,
ENTITLED *ISIS*,
WAS ORIGINALLY GIVEN BY THE
ACTOR SACHA GUITRY
TO HIS SON.

Le Musée de la Marine
The Maritime Museum

Palais de Chaillot
75016 Paris
Tel: (01) 45-53-31-70

Open every day except Tuesday
10:00 A.M. to 6:00 P.M.

Metro: Trocadéro
Bus: 22, 30, 32, 63, 72, 82

THESE EXQUISITELY CARVED
IVORY SHIP MODELS ARE AMONG THE
UNUSUAL OBJECTS
AT THE MARITIME MUSEUM;
THE ONE IN THE FOREGROUND
WAS MADE BY
FRENCH PRISONERS INCARCERATED
IN ENGLAND DURING
THE NAPOLEONIC WARS (1794–1817).

IN 1810, a dazzling seventeen-meter-long ceremonial State Barge was built in a record twenty-one days for the French Emperor Napóleon Bonaparte. Painted white and gold, and outfitted with a small deck-side cabin topped with the imperial crown, the barge was only used once by Napóleon and the Empress Marie-Louise, during an inspection of the Antwerp dockyard that same year. Eventually moved to the naval dockyard at Brest, the sumptuous vessel sailed for the last time during a 1922 parade of the French naval school. Miraculously spared from the bombings of Brest, the ceremonial boat was transferred to Paris by horse-drawn barge and wagon at the height of World War II. Still, its trials were far from over. Only after an opening was made in the side of the Palais de Chaillot, could the lengthy boat be installed in the new Maritime Museum in July 1945, where it has been "docked" ever since.

It is worth a visit to the Maritime Museum just to see this remarkable vessel. However, few people realize that this museum, which was created in 1830 (making it one of the oldest in France), contains an unrivaled collection of French wooden ship models from the seventeenth and eighteenth centuries that are marvels of craftsmanship, as well as precious historical documents.

That these models exist at all, is due in part to the French King Louis XIV and his Minister Colbert, who commissioned the French royal shipyards to build and maintain flawless miniature replicas of the navy's five classes of military galleys, which could

later serve as prototypes for future naval construction. Many of the ship-yards' administrative officers took the opportunity to build their own collections of ship models, the most famous being that of Duhamel de Monceau, the General Inspector of the French Navy. Unable to preserve his staggering accumulation of vessels, frigates, galleys, cargo-boats, and nautical equipment in his own residence, Duhamel de Monceau presented it to the French king, who transferred it to the Louvre.

Once there, the collection lay virtually forgotten until it caught the attention of the French Navy's Chief Admiral, Louis-Antoine de Bourbon, who was also the eldest son of Charles X. Because of de Bourbon's yearning to present this rich hoard of nautical objects to a wider audience, Charles X decreed that a new naval museum should be organized within the precincts of the Louvre and opened to the general public. France's first naval museum, the Musée Dauphin (named after the Prince de Bourbon), opened its doors to the public in January 1830.

Only a few months later, the July Revolution of 1830 not only caused Charles X and his family to flee, but also resulted in some minor vandalism inside the museum. Despite this setback, the naval museum remained firmly ensconced in the Louvre for the next 109 years, where its collec-tions were continuously enriched, before being relocated to the Palais de Chaillot during World War II.

The museum's imaginative curatorial staff has taken great pains to show every facet of maritime activity, from war to trade, through displays of authentic objects that make the rich and complex history of navigation come alive before the visitor's eyes. Whether one is a sailor or a landlubber, the exhibits arouse one's desire to learn, as well as to dream. Seeing the breathtaking replica of the *Ocean* at the entrance of the museum—a six-and-a-half-meter-high replica of a three-decker with 120 cannons and all its sails—it is easy to find oneself captivated by the boat's intricate design and by visions of what life may have been like aboard, on the vast and often treacherous ocean.

Among the rarest and most beautiful wooden ship models are those representing the French military galley, which attained its zenith during the reigns of Louis XIII and Louis XIV. Looking at these exquisitely made models, particularly *La Dauphine*, the only extant example of a "galley extraordinary," or the splendid *Réale*, it is difficult to see these boats as dreaded floating prisons, manned by convicts and slaves who were chained to rowing benches.

It would be a pity to overlook the museum's most sumptuous models, notable for their elaborate and often exquisite carvings and detail. There is the *Louis XV*, most likely built for the king in 1720–25 by a veteran craftsman whose nostalgia for the glories of the past caused him to embellish this 110-gun three-decker with an excess of ornamentation and gold leaf, outmoded by the time the young monarch assumed the throne.

The museum's exhibits indicate that the French Navy's most glorious period was during the American War of Independence. The handsome wooden model of the *Artésien*, a sixty-four-gun ship first launched in 1765, is a small-scale version of the actual vessel that was used in French naval warfare during this memorable, albeit brief, epoch.

So proud was Louis XVI of France's victories over the British dur-

THIS "FIRE-BREATHING" CHINESE BRONZE CANNON
REPRESENTING A DRAGON
WAS TAKEN FROM A CITADEL THAT ONCE PROTECTED
THE ENTRANCE TO THE PORT OF CHÂU DOC
(NOW IN SOUTH VIETNAM).

ing the American Revolution, that he commissioned a series of sixteen paintings by the Marquis of Rossel commemorating the war's principal sea battles to adorn the naval academies at Brest, Rochefort, and Toulon. Two of the works, which are displayed in the museum's main gallery, *The Battle of the Belle-Poule Against the HMS Arethuse* and *The Battle of the Lisbonne*, while pictorially naïve, nonetheless provide a valuable document of the war's vessels and sea skirmishes.

Without a doubt, the most out-standing paintings in the museum's collection are those of Joseph Vernet (1714–1789), regarded as one of France's finest nautical painters. Vernet, who had studied in Italy for twenty years, earned such a considerable reputation that, in 1752, Louis XVI commissioned him to paint the principal ports of France, including Toulon, Brest, Bordeaux,

Dieppe, Marseilles, and Le Havre. For ten years, from 1754 to 1764, Vernet moved from port to port with his family, executing a total of fifteen canvases, thirteen of which are in this museum. While the core of the Maritime Museum is its marvelous collection of sailing-ship models, it is also notable for its rich and comprehensive displays showing the beginnings of steam and the history of the great ocean liners, such as the *Normandie* and the *France*. Equally impressive is its fine collection of historic navigational instruments and underwater diving gear, the latter dating back to the nineteenth century.

The museum demonstrates that many navigational inventions were often initially spurned, needlessly retarding progress. The best example of this is the invention of the steam-powered sailing vessel. Denis Papin, the French Protestant scientist and inventor who was the first to recognize the power of steam in 1690, successfully tested a steamboat on wheels as early as 1707 in the Fulde River in Germany. However, after the jealous ferrymen destroyed Papin's prototype, the discouraged inventor gave up, and died penniless.

In 1783, the Marquis Claude de Jouffroy-d'Abbans tested a steamboat with a single-cylinder engine—whose model is now on display in the museum—which made its way upstream on the River Saône for a quarter of an hour. Although the trial was witnessed by a considerable crowd and was the subject of an official inquiry, the French Academy of Sciences deemed the results unsatisfactory, thereby allowing a remarkable development to slip away. Even Robert Fulton, who successfully tested his steamboat *The Clermont* on the Seine in 1803, failed to interest Napoléon in his invention.

A CLOSE-UP OF *THE OCEAN*.

A FULLY-RIGGED MODEL OF
THE OCEAN,
ONE-SIXTEENTH THE SIZE OF
THE ORIGINAL SHIP,
GREETS VISITORS AT THE ENTRANCE
TO THE MARITIME MUSEUM.

Undaunted by this snub, he returned to the United States, where, in 1806, he established the first steamboat company, with service between New York and Albany.

Among the most affecting exhibits at the Maritime Museum is the collection of objects from the ill-fated shipwreck of the La Pérouse expedition, found on Vanikoro, a Pacific island northeast of New Caledonia, where the French explorer's ships, *L'Astrolabe (The Astrolabe)* and *La Boussole (The Compass)*, were wrecked in 1788. Three years earlier, at the behest of Louis XVI, these ships had set sail with 223 sailors and 21 scientists, as well as 950 tons of nautical and scientific material, to explore the Pacific. Seeing the humble tools from these shipwrecked vessels, it is moving to think of the brave men who risked their lives on the high seas on the other side of the globe, until the final onslaught of a hurricane shattered their boat and drowned them in the middle of the night, not far from one of the last undiscovered islands on earth.

A visit to the Maritime Museum provides an opportunity to gain a better understanding of the thrilling history of navigation, as well as of the fascinating personalities and events that shaped it. Even though the closing years of this century are focused on the conquest of outer space, and on organizing the road map of tomorrow's information highways, this museum is an invaluable reminder of how much we owe to the diligent shipbuilders, tenacious inventors, and intrepid explorers of our seas and oceans.

NAPOLEON BONAPARTE ONLY SAILED ONCE IN THIS REMARKABLE STATE BARGE (TO INSPECT THE ANTWERP DOCKYARD IN 1810).

A CLOSE-UP OF ONE OF THE MARITIME MUSEUM'S FAMED COPPER-BOTTOM SHIP MODELS, *LA FOUDROYANTE (THE THUNDERER)*.

Le Musée de l'Institut du Monde Arabe

The Museum of the Institute of the Arab World

1, Rue des Fossés Saint-Bernard
75005 Paris
Tel: (01) 40–51–39–53

Open every day except Monday
10:00 A.M. to 6:00 P.M.

Metro: Jussieu, Cardinal-Lemoine
Bus: 24, 63, 67, 86, 87, 89

Rooftop restaurant, cafeteria.

THE FAÇADE OF THE
INSTITUTE OF THE ARAB WORLD;
A STUNNING BLEND OF
MODERN WESTERN AND TRADITIONAL
MOORISH ARCHITECTURE.

WHEN ONE thinks of the *grands travaux* (great works) of the 1980s, what usually springs to mind are the *Grand Louvre* and the *Musée d'Orsay*, along with the *Grande Arche* at *La Défense* and the four book-shaped towers of the *Bibliothèque de France* at Bercy.

Often overlooked is the much-acclaimed headquarters of the Institute of the Arab World designed by Jean Nouvel, Pierre Soria, Gilbert Lezenes, and the Architecture Studio (Martin Robin, Jean-François Galmiche, Rodo Tisnado, and Jean-François Bonne), which was opened to the public in 1987. This stunning steel and glass building located at the beginning of the Boulevard Saint-Germain is the only structure ever built in Paris whose conscious aim was to unite Arab and Western cultural influences.

If this unique building salutes the architecture of two cultures, it is in keeping with the aims of the Institute of the Arab World, a French cultural foundation whose overriding objectives are to encourage and develop the study and understanding of the Arab world in France and to promote cultural exchange. It is important to note that the Institute boasts a lively program of activities including film festivals, lectures, and colloquia offered by leading scholars from all over the globe.

Three floors of this building have been allocated to the permanent collection of the Museum of the Institute of the Arab World, which reveals the art, culture, and civilization of the Arab-Islamic area, both prior to and after the advent of

THIS TALL, CYLINDRICAL BOX OF EBONY,
DECORATED WITH
SILVER AND CALLIGRAPHY,
HOLDS THE SCROLLS OF THE KORAN.
IT WAS MADE DURING THE SECOND HALF OF THE
NINETEENTH CENTURY IN TURKEY.

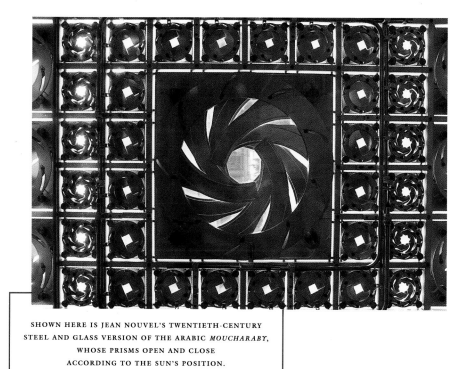

Islam. (Four other levels have been set aside for temporary expositions.)

While most people tend to associate Arab culture mainly with countries in the Middle East, the Institute's intention is to champion the art and ethnography of all the nations in the Arab League: Algeria, Saudi Arabia, Bahrain, Djibouti, Egypt, the United Arab Emirates, Iraq, Jordan, Kuwait, Lebanon, Libya, Morocco, Mauritania, Oman, Qatar, Somalia, Sudan, Tunisia, and Yemen.

"In light of current and past political events both within and outside of France, the vision of Arabic culture is somewhat narrow," notes chief curator Catherine Vaudour. "Many people don't realize the importance of this culture throughout history, or that it is a civilization which spread far beyond the Mediterranean all the way to Persia and India. Our intention is to broaden the general public's understanding of Arabic culture, so that the term 'Arab' loses its pejorative aspect. It's important that people know that the Arab world was rich and powerful—in fact, extraordinary."

To that end, the museum displays a collection of artifacts, architectural fragments, sculptures, ceramics, costumes, jewelry, carpets, manuscripts, and scientific instruments that trace the major epochs in Arab history, from prehistoric times all the way to the nineteenth century.

To amplify and enhance its existing collection, last fall the museum opened its "Museum of Arab Museums," allotting display space for the first time to objects selected from the reserves of Arab institutions, on loan for three years. The project has made it possible to add a total of 180 objects—130 from Tunisia and 50 from Syria—most of which have never been displayed in Europe before.

THE ROOFTOP TERRACE OF THE INSTITUTE OF THE ARAB WORLD WITH ITS SPLENDID PANORAMIC VIEW OF PARIS, INCLUDING THE TOWERS OF NÔTRE-DAME.

"This project offers a new insight into the culture of the Arab world," notes Vaudour. "By establishing a partnership with these museums and their curators, who have had a central role in the selection of these objects, we have created a different sort of dialogue."

That dialogue begins on the museum's seventh floor, and works downward to the sixth and fourth floors, which is an unusual arrangement when compared with other institutions. The museum also takes a giant step forward by showing that the heritage of the Arab world starts not with the advent and rise of Islam, but with the Paleolithic and Neolithic eras. Displays of primitive flints and other stone-cutting tools, followed by displays of Greek-and Roman-influenced pottery, perfume burners, and death masks, as well as statuary and mosaics on the seventh floor,

demonstrate the rich and complex civilization of early Arabia that goes back to the first millennium B.C.

Although an arid and inhospitable land, Northern Arabia was also a crossroads of international trade, as reflected in the international cities of Petra and Palmyra. Vassals of Rome, these Arab kingdoms gave birth to two emperors during the third century B.C., Elagabalus, and Philip the Arab, as well as to Greek- and Roman-inspired art and architecture, evident in the museum's displays that include statues of bare-breasted men and women.

The vast expanses of Central Arabia engendered two ways of life: that of the desert and the tribe and that of the oasis and the city. This desert civilization, typified by the Bedouin, depended upon ideals of courage, honor, and hospitality. In ancient times, a polytheistic religion was practiced, in which invisible beings, *djinns* or genies, played an important role.

The Islamic period officially began in A.D. 622 after the Prophet Muhammad was forced into exile by the notables of Mecca, eventually coming to Medina, "the city of the Prophet," and establishing the first mosque in his own home. An organizer, strategist and political leader, Muhammad developed the notion of the *ummah,* a community uniting tribes and clans around a religious ideal. Although he conquered his native city Mecca in A.D. 630, he died without a direct male descendant and without having ordained a successor. From A.D. 632 to A.D. 660, four Caliphs, "successors to the messenger of God," directed the new Arab state and conducted the first wave of conquests.

While the museum does not document or illustrate the rise and dissemination of Islam, its exhibits, notably on the sixth and fourth floors, demonstrate the way the arts and sciences flourished during the Umayyad and Abbasid dynasties, as well as during the Mameluke and Ottoman Empires.

Although the span of the Umayyad dynasty, the first hereditary dynasty of Islam, was brief, lasting a little over a century (A.D. 661–A.D. 750), it encompassed the Arab nation's greatest territorial conquests and gave birth to Muslim art. Even as its architecture borrowed from conquered civilizations, its interpretation of the Koranic injunction against the representation of God compelled artists to replace human figures with floral, geometric, and epigraphic motifs.

A FRAGMENT OF A THIRTEENTH-CENTURY
CARVED WOODEN CORBEL
FROM TOLEDO, SPAIN.

AN EIGHTEENTH-CENTURY KORANIC SCROLL, PAINTED WITH INK,
GOUACHE, AND GOLD, WAS MADE DURING THE OTTOMAN EMPIRE.
(COURTESY MUSÉE DE L'INSTITUT DU MONDE ARABE).

Coins, including gold dinars and silver dirhams with Arabic inscriptions, as well as rare examples of pottery from the Umayyad period, are displayed on a bed of sand inside a hanging glass case embellished with a serigraph of the Grand Mosque in Damascus, built between A.D. 705 and A.D. 715.

In A.D. 750, a descendant of Muhammad's uncle, Al-Abbas, seized power and had all the members of the Umayyad dynasty massacred with the exception of the Prince 'Abd ar-Rahman, who fled to Spain and founded the Emirate of Cordoba, a brilliant cultural center that was to last until 1031. With the founding of the Abbasid dynasty, the empire's center was transferred to Iraq. Baghdad became the new capital, a center of culture and science, as well as great wealth, exemplified by the Caliph Hārūn ar-Rashid, a contemporary of Charlemagne, who was celebrated in the *One Thousand and One Nights*.

Fragments of sculptured wood and stone decorations that once ornamented mosques and palaces, as well as ceramic tiles, pottery and lusterware, art forms first widely developed during the Abbasid dynasty, are allocated an important place among the museum's exhibits.

The world owes a large debt to the Abbasid rulers, in particular Hārūn ar-Rashid and his successor Al-Ma'mun, who through Baghdad's Bayt al-Hikma (House of Wisdom) encouraged scholars of all origins and religions to work together. The use of paper (a factory was established in Baghdad as of A.D. 894) facilitated the spread of ideas. Arabic was not only at one time the international scientific language, it also had an impact on English, introducing such words as cipher, algebra, alcohol, alkali, almanac, zenith, and zero.

Instruments and manuscripts in the museum's display cases illustrate this flourishing era of Arabic research and scientific breakthroughs in the fields of mathematics (weights and measures), astronomy (celestial globes, astrolabes, compasses and sundials), and medicine (mortars and vessels for pharmacopoeia).

A high point of the museum is a magnificent collection of astrolabes from the tenth to the seventeenth centuries, donated by Marcel Destombes. Displayed against the sky of Paris, they allow the visitor to imagine how an astronomer once held them at arm's length in his observatory.

The Museum of the Institute of the Arab World contains a precious legacy which not only helps to illuminate the past, but also enhances our understanding of many current advances we may have come to take for granted. Its handsome and well-documented displays of sumptuous woven rugs and textiles, richly embroidered costumes, ceramics and scientific instruments, confirm that without the influence of Arabic art and science, the world as we know it today would be a very different place.

THIS RARE ASTROLABE
WAS CREATED BY
IBRAHIM MUHAMMAD AL-BALAWI
IN 1686–87.

Le Musée de la Monnaie

The Museum of Coins and Medallions

**11, Quai de Conti
75006 Paris
Tel: (01) 40-46-55-35**

**Open every day except Monday
from 1:00 P.M. to 6:00 P.M.;
Wednesday evenings until 9:00 P.M.**

**Metro: Pont Neuf, Odéon
Bus: 24, 27, 58, 70**

THE MUSEUM OF COINS AND
MEDALLIONS IS LOCATED IN THIS
IMPRESSIVE BUILDING
OVERLOOKING THE SEINE.
ITS STUNNING NEOCLASSICAL FACADE
IS ORNAMENTED WITH
SIX ALLEGORICAL FIGURES BY
THE FINEST SCULPTORS OF THE PERIOD,
INCLUDING JEAN-BAPTISTE PIGALLE
AND HIS NEPHEW
LOUIS-PHILIPPE MOUCHY.

OPPOSITE THE oldest bridge in Paris, the Pont Neuf, and the Louvre Museum, stands one of the most imposing and impressive edifices in Paris: the Hôtel de la Monnaie, the architectural masterpiece of Jacques-Denis Antoine, and home of the French Mint from 1775 to 1973. Although the building was commissioned by Louis XV, it was only completed after his death. The mathematician and philosopher, the Marquis de Condorcet, who was appointed Inspector General of the Mint by Louis XVI's finance minister Turgot, lived here for fifteen years. It was also in this building that his wife, Sophie de Grouchy, presided over a brilliant salon frequented by such luminaries as Thomas Jefferson, Benjamin Franklin, Adam Smith, and Pierre-Auguste Beaumarchais (author of *The Barber of Seville* and *The Marriage of Figaro*).

THROUGH THIS ARCHWAY ONE CAN SEE THE
COUR D'HONNEUR AND THE DOORWAY OF THE MUSEUM OF COINS
AND MEDALLIONS, ONCE HOME TO THE FRENCH MINT.
ABOVE THE PORTALS ARE THE FRENCH ROYAL COAT OF ARMS
SURROUNDED BY THE FEMALE
ALLEGORICAL FIGURES OF GOODWILL AND ABUNDANCE.

THE ENTRANCE TO
THE MUSEUM OF COINS AND MEDALLIONS,
THROUGH WHICH ONE CAN SEE
ITS MONUMENTAL DORIC COLUMNS.

THE CABINET AND PORTRAIT OF ONE
OF FRANCE'S MOST RENOWNED ENGRAVERS,
JACQUES-JEAN BARRE (1793–1855),
DIRECTOR OF ENGRAVINGS
AT THE FRENCH MINT FROM 1843 TO 1855.

Since 1988, this magnificent building has been the premises of the Museum of Coins and Medallions. Don't be misled by its imposing and stately exterior: inside is an elegant, inviting museum considered to be among the most modern in the world. Instead of displaying coins in traditional vitrines, the museum's architects have chosen to insert coins and medals into luminous freestanding glass and metal walls, making it possible to see both faces of each piece. To enhance a visitor's appreciation of the evolution of money and coinage, the curators have installed a sophisticated audiovisual system on the ground floor, which offers a highly informative and fascinating presentation of the history of French coinage from the fifth century B.C. to the modern era.

What makes this museum so exceptional is that, through its

A SCULPTURE OF THE GODDESS OF FORTUNE
BY LOUIS-PHILIPPE MOUCHY (1734-1801)
PRESIDES OVER THIS MACHINE
ONCE USED FOR STRIKING MEDALS
DURING THE REIGN OF KING LOUIS XIV.

displays of 2,000 coins spanning fifteen centuries, its stunning collection of 450 commemorative and artistic medals dating back to the Renaissance, as well as its exhibits of numismatic tools and machinery, visitors learn not only about the chronology of coinage but also of its wide-ranging impact on people and society.

"The Musée de la Monnaie was conceived as a place where a story unfolds, where we explain how people, in order to fulfill their activities, needed to find a means of exchange, and how—in order to do so—they invented objects that represented their buying power and their fortune," notes Evelyne Cohen, the museum's curator.

"We also show how these same coins were used to communicate the images and ideology of the state," she continues. "We should remember

that Louis XVI was caught during his flight to Varennes because a man recognized the king from the royal image on the copper coins he used every day."

The museum's self-guided tour begins by showing how money first made its appearance in Gaul 300 years before the birth of Christ, and how the first Celtic coins were inspired by Greek and Roman models (with a bent toward fantasy), featuring stylized human heads and horses. After having been defeated by Julius Caesar during the first century A.D., the conquered Gauls gradually adopted the Roman system used throughout the Empire.

During the Middle Ages, with the impoverishment of Western Europe, gold coins began to disappear from circulation. The Emperor Charlemagne (A.D. 768–A.D. 814) created a monetary system based on a silver standard that was to last for a thousand years in Europe: one *livre* (about 400 grams of silver in the beginning) equalled 20 *sous* or 240 *deniers*. Until 1970, the British pound sterling was divided into 20 shillings (20 sous), each of which was worth 12 pence (abbreviated *d*. for deniers). It was also under Charlemagne that the first mint was established in Paris.

However, as the museum's exhibits demonstrate, this monetary stability was not to last in France. Confronted by the problems of succession, menaced by Hungarian, Saracen, and Norman invasions, the Carolingian kings were no longer able to govern. The wealthy and powerful nobility from Champagne, Flanders, Burgundy, and Normandy—who now had territories much vaster than the king's—were each able to issue separate currencies, to their great profit.

At last, during the economic expansion in the eleventh and twelfth centuries, the French monarch Philippe Auguste (reigned 1180–1223) was able to consolidate his power and issue coins that would be used throughout his kingdom—the *denier tournois*.

Under the reign of Saint Louis (1226–70) France became a powerful and prosperous nation, and international trade assumed an even greater importance. It was at this time that Louis issued the silver *gros* or *sou tournois*, (equal to 12 *deniers*, it was the first French sou in circulation). He also circulated a gold *écu*, the first gold coin to be minted since the ninth century. Extremely rare, there are only eight such coins in existence, one of which is on display in the museum.

Although the Hundred Years War was fraught with economic and political dislocation, during this period the battered French monarchy issued some exceptionally beautiful gold coins—masterpieces in Gothic engraving—as a means of enhancing its diminished prestige.

In 1360 the *franc* made its appearance for the first time, as a gold coin representing Jean le Bon (reigned 1350–1364) dressed in military armor on horseback. This coin was minted after France's defeat at Poitiers, and after Jean le Bon was freed by the English in exchange for a ransom of 3 million gold écus (about 3,500 kilos of gold)! The term *franc* meant that the king was *franc des Anglais* (freed from the English).

THESE TOOLS FOR ENGRAVING
MEDALLIONS,
WHICH ONCE BELONGED TO
JACQUES-JEAN BARRE,
A DIRECTOR OF ENGRAVINGS
AT THE FRENCH MINT,
DIFFER LITTLE FROM THOSE
USED TODAY.

Still, it was only after Napoléon Bonaparte established *le franc germinal* in 1803, equal to the livre under Louis XV and Louis XVI, that the French monetary system was finally based on the *franc* instead of the *livre*. (The first franc under the French Republic, was minted on August 15, 1795.) Despite all the ensuing political upheaval during the nineteenth century, France enjoyed great monetary stability until 1914, with the franc's weight in silver remaining virtually unchanged.

In addition to presenting a comprehensive overview of the history of the French monetary system, the Museum of Coins and Medallions displays illustrations of the early techniques for making coins and medals. Finely painted sixteenth-century Swiss stained-glass windows demonstrate the painstaking labor that went into making coins by hand. Metal was first heated, then melted, then cut into round circles, then hammered into coins, and finally engraved by hand. Each coin was scrupulously checked to ensure that the proper weight was maintained. Counterfeiters could be put to death (the common punishment was to boil the guilty party in a cauldron!).

Fortunately, by the middle of the sixteenth century, technicians had succeeded in developing a hand-operated machine for striking money, which made it possible to mint coins and medals mechanically, thus ensuring that money had a consistent weight and quality. This critical invention increased the speed of minting and stopped the practice of trimming off and stealing precious metal from each minted coin, a fraudulent practice in effect since antiquity.

The museum's exhibits also include a series of machines showing the evolution of the French Mint, including a manual coin and medal press from the reign of Louis XIV, a press made with the melted bronze from Russian cannons captured at the Battle of Austerlitz (1805), and the oldest known steam-operated press, made in 1830, which averaged fifteen pieces a minute.

Also on display is a stunning collection of medallions. The museum's audiovisual presentation recounts how medal portraiture first developed as a highly prized art form in Italy, largely through the initiative of court painter and medallist Antonio Pisanello (1395–1455).

Under the reigns of both Louis XIV and Napoléon Bonaparte, the medal was used as an instrument of propaganda. The museum's extensive display reveals how medals have provided miniature records of some of the most significant events in history. Perhaps one of the most impressive exhibits is the series of medals depicting key events of the French Revolution, including the taking of the Bastille, the eradication of privileges, the meeting of the Estates General, and the beheading of Marie-Antoinette. It's amazing to think that these small circles of metal, some no more than a half inch in diameter, chronicled day-by-day the joys, dreams, deceptions, and pride of a people.

Today, the French Mint continues to be the world's leading producer of artistic and commemorative medals, all of which are still made by hand in ateliers in the same building housing the museum. In an ongoing program, over a hundred outside artists have collaborated on designs, including Salvador Dalí, Georges Mathieu, and César.

After touring the Museum of Coins and Medallions, it's impossible to think of coins or medals as only remote, inanimate objects. With the assistance of the documentation now

A MARBLE BUST OF NAPOLÉON
BY ANTONIO CANOVA (1757–1822).

available at this museum, these
objects—be they of gold, silver,
copper, brass, or nickel—can be used
as a means of better comprehending
our own lives and those of others,
both past and present.

Le Musée de Montmartre

The Museum of Montmartre

12, Rue Cortot
75018 Paris
Tel: (01) 46–06–61–11

Open Tuesday through Sunday
11:00 A.M. to 6:00 P.M.

Metro: Lamarck-Caulaincourt,
Pigalle
Bus: 64, 80

THE MUSEUM OF MONTMARTRE
IS LOCATED IN A
SEVENTEENTH-CENTURY DWELLING
THAT WAS ONCE HOME
TO THE ACTOR ROSIMOND,
A MEMBER OF MOLIÈRE'S TROUPE.

V ISITORS WHO see the Place du Tertre and the Sacré Coeur crowded with tourists and souvenir shops may wonder if this is the Montmartre that has long been known as a gathering place for poets, painters, writers, and musicians. They needn't worry. The proof they seek is very much in evidence at the charming Museum of Montmartre, located atop the slope of the last existing vineyard in Paris, where a harvest is celebrated annually on the first Saturday in October.

The museum, open since 1979, is in a seventeenth-century residence, once occupied by the actor Rose de Rosimond (Claude de la Rose), a member of Molière's troupe, who—like his mentor—died on stage during a performance of *Le Malade Imaginaire* (*The Hypochondriac*). When Rosimond resided here

Montmartre was not considered part of Paris; only in 1860 did it become the city's eighteenth district.

During the last quarter of the nineteenth century, this large white edifice and garden was both a residence and atelier for a coterie of painters, including Maurice Utrillo, Suzanne Valadon, Raoul Dufy, Francisque Poulbot, and Pierre-Auguste Renoir.

Sitting in the verdant bower leading to the museum, where only the sounds of chirping birds can be heard, it's easy to imagine Renoir at his easel painting *The Garden of the Rue Cortot in Montmartre* (1876), a work that now hangs in Pittsburgh's Carnegie-Mellon Institute.

Although there are no great works of art at the Museum of Montmartre, there is a treasure trove of pictures, posters, photographs, manuscripts, and objects documenting the two-thousand-year history of this unique locale.

"Our goal with this museum is to acquaint people with the culture of Montmartre," explains the museum's director, Jean-Marc Tarrit. "We want the public to know the history of this area that extends back to the Romans. The wealth of the Montmartre Museum resides in its diversity of artifacts, rather than in its art collection. Our goal is to preserve the history of Montmartre, as well as Montmartre itself."

It is here that one can learn that the highest point in Paris was once the site of two Roman temples, later converted into a Celtic shrine. In 1133, the Church of Saint-Pierre de Montmartre was built on the site as part of a Benedictine abbey founded by King Louis VI and his wife, Adélaïde of Savoie, the first abbess to be buried there. Although the church still exists, the abbey was destroyed during the French Revolution.

THIS VINEYARD, ADJACENT TO THE MUSEUM OF MONTMARTRE, WAS PLANTED IN 1933. A HARVEST IS CELEBRATED ANNUALLY ON THE FIRST SATURDAY IN OCTOBER.

Using authentic documents from the period, the museum relates the tragic fate of the last abbess, Marie-Louise de Montmorency-Laval, who was guillotined along with fifteen other women from the religious order. Although the abbess was both deaf and blind at the time of her trial, her condition proved no deterrent to her accusers, who condemned her to death for treason. Her prosecutor was reported to have said at the trial: "It's fine, it's fine. Write that she conspired blindly and deafly."

Thanks to the photographer Louis-Emile Durandelle, as well as to an unparalleled collection of period drawings and sketches, it is possible to get a vivid impression of the building of the Church of Sacré-Coeur, erected between 1875 and 1919. Over seventy-eight proposals were

submitted for the edifice; first prize went to Paul Abadie (1812–1884), an architect from the Rationalist School, and an ardent disciple of Viollet-le-Duc. Much like the Eiffel Tower, Sacré-Coeur had its share of opponents, including leading political figures (among them France's future prime minister Georges Clemenceau).

When Sacré-Coeur's builders weren't fighting off the opposition—the construction site was almost impounded in 1906—they were carrying out the arduous task of creating solid foundations for the massive building. Digging forty-five meters into the ground, the church's builders erected eighty-three pillars, each one placed in holes that reached down to solid ground, which were then filled in with masonry, gravel, and lime. Joined together by a series of underground arcades, the pillars supported the walls and columns of the edifice. In the end, 35,000 cubic meters of masonry replaced 35,000 cubic meters of earth, causing one bishop to remark that even if the summit of Montmartre were to crumble, the basilica of Sacré-Coeur would remain standing.

The museum's exhibits show that Montmartre's windy position made it an ideal spot for both windmills and hot-air balloons. At one time, the area included a total of eighteen windmills that were used for crushing stone for plaster, dyes for perfumery, and grains for flour. In 1814, four millers, known as the Debray brothers, led a heroic fight to oppose the armies of the Coalition against Napoléon. Legend has it that Pierre-Charles Debray, pierced by a Cossack's lance, was suspended from the wings of his mill. His son, who was both a miller and a wine-merchant, transformed the first mill into a *guinguette* (restaurant with dancing) and organized the first public ball for the youth of Montmartre. It was also here that the first hot *galette* (flat cake) was sold. This cake would later inspire the name of *Le Moulin de la Galette*, which was opened as a public dance hall in 1871.

The museum also shows how well-known Montmartre was for its quarries, which—at one time—extended over a quarter of the steep hillside referred to as *La Butte*. First utilized by the Romans, these quarries were exploited for their limestone and gypsum (the latter was referred to as "montmartrite"). In the nineteenth century, these quarries were still furnishing Paris with three-fourths of the plaster it required.

These same quarries were repositories for all sorts of fossils, some of which were collected by the French naturalist Georges Cuvier (1769–1832). Studying this unknown fauna, which included turtles, crocodiles, and certain mammals, Cuvier pioneered a new science—paleontology. When he found a fossil of what he presumed to be the "oldest Montmartrois," he named it *adapis pariensis*, mistakenly thinking the animal's bone came from a steer. Twenty years ago, another paleontologist identified the bone as actually being that of a human ancestor.

Still, when most people think of Montmartre, it isn't the study of fossils that comes to mind, but the frenzied and often unruly nightlife of its cabarets: *Le Chat Noir, Le Moulin Rouge, Le Moulin de la Galette*, and *Le Lapin Agile*. This collection pays fond tribute to them all.

Although the museum contains a number of vivid paintings of Montmartre nightlife by minor artists, one work stands out above the rest: Toulouse-Lautrec's original 1891 poster of *La Goulue* (Louise Weber) and her partner *Valentin le Désossé*

PARCE DOMINE, BY ADOLPHE WILLETTE.
(COURTESY MUSÉE DE MONTMARTRE, PARIS.)

(Jules Renaudin) kicking up their heels at the *Moulin Rouge*. A wonderful collection of menus, postcards, and photographs provides a glimpse of the cabaret's spirited gaiety, which united upper and lower classes for the first time.

Of course, Montmartre was also known for its bistros. The French language borrowed that word from the Cossacks who demanded that their meals at *La Mère Catherine* (a restaurant still in existence) be served *bistro*, meaning "fast" in Russian.

To capture the atmosphere of a typical Montmartre bistro, the museum has recreated the decor of the *Bistro de l'Abreuvoir*—one of Utrillo's favorite watering holes—with its original oak and zinc counter and wooden tables. It is the only antique *zinc* left in Paris, since the Germans seized the metal counters during World War II and melted them down for weapons.

The museum also pays homage to many of Montmartre's famous residents, including the composers Hector Berlioz and Darius Milhaud, the poets Gérard de Nerval and Max

Jacob, as well as the painters Maurice Utrillo, Suzanne Valadon, and Jules Pascin. Their watercolors, drawings, and photographs, as well as manuscripts and letters, reveal how their bohemian existence was often a mingling of misery and achievement, pain and triumph.

Perhaps the prize for the most idiosyncratic creation at the museum goes to the photographic reproduction of a painting ascribed to Joachim-Raphael Boronali. Roland Dorgelès, a novelist who took issue with the painters of the Bateau-Lavoir, thought the best way to debunk modern art was to tie a paintbrush to the tail of Lolo, the donkey that belonged to Frédéric Gérard, the proprietor of the *Lapin Agile*. Lolo's "seascape," entitled *Sunset Over the Adriatic* and attributed to Boronali, was exhibited at the Salon des Indépendants and purchased by a collector for 500 francs.

While this so-called "work of art" may be judged worthless, the sort of ironic and independent spirit that inspired it is inestimable. In an era of increasing homogenization and

conformity, the Museum of
Montmartre is a precious reminder
that this celebrated Parisian locale has
been a fertile ground for a unique
blend of individualism and talent that
has made its indelible mark on the
world.

Le Musée Gustave Moreau

The Gustave Moreau Museum

14, Rue de La Rochefoucauld
75009 Paris
Tel: (01) 48-74-38-50

Open Monday and Wednesday
from 11:00 A.M. to 5:15 P.M.;
Thursday, Friday, Saturday, and
Sunday from 10:00 A.M. to Noon
and from 2:00 P.M. to 5:15 P.M.

Metro: Trinité
Bus: 26, 32, 43, 49

AS EVERYONE knows, the preservation of artists' homes and ateliers has generally resulted from the munificence and diligence of state-supported institutions, admirers, and inheritors. That is why it may come as a surprise to learn that the renowned French Symbolist painter Gustave Moreau (1826–1898) personally orchestrated the transformation of his family's mansion in Paris's Nouvelle-Athènes area into a museum commemorating his life and work.

Moreover, this is no ordinary museum. Just the way celebrities carefully craft their public image, Moreau was determined to present and preserve one of his own. For his museum, he meticulously enshrined the memorabilia of those dearest to him and organized the display of almost 6,000 of his paintings, watercolors, and drawings: works attesting to a lifelong quest to create the ideal painting of his age—a deliberate throwback to the Renaissance.

As early as 1862, when Moreau was thirty-six years old, he confided to his journal a concern for how his work would be perceived after he was gone: "Tonight, I think of my death and of the fate of my humble works, and of all those compositions that I have taken pains to put together; separated, they perish; taken together, they give a small idea of the kind of artist I was and of the atmosphere in which I liked to dream."

Not a man to gamble with destiny, in 1895 Moreau commissioned architect Albert Lafon (1860–1935) to transform the private house left to him by his family into a museum that

A VIEW OF ONE
OF GUSTAVE MOREAU'S
CLUTTERED ATELIERS.

THIS ORNATE STAIRCASE,
BUILT TO MOREAU'S SPECIFICATIONS,
JOINS THE UPSTAIRS AND DOWNSTAIRS
STUDIOS WHERE MOST OF HIS
PAINTINGS AND DRAWINGS ARE DISPLAYED.

would contain two large ateliers with immense windows facing north, wherein fifty years of his work would be displayed. He also commissioned Lafon to build a stunning, freestanding wrought-iron spiral staircase joining the third and fourth floors of the museum. Visitors to the museum today will find that almost every inch of the ateliers' salmon pink walls are covered with Moreau's paintings, and that their placement was often designated by the artist himself. Moreover, along the northern side of the ateliers beneath the windows are unusual wall cabinets, which when open reveal series after series of Moreau's drawings and watercolors framed under glass and hung on moveable hinges.

One element that deserves special attention in this atypical museum is a large square wood-and-glass-topped cabinet, whose four sides open up to reveal an extraordinary collection of 123 small-scale paintings and watercolors, revealing the work of an artist whose inexhaustible imagination embraced landscapes, portraits, and fables, as well as themes from the Bible and mythology.

Although Moreau was notoriously shy and highly sensitive to any sort of criticism—to such an extent that he essentially stopped exhibiting after 1880—he nonetheless chose to convert the second floor of his museum into a symbolic residence filled with his family's furnishings and memorabilia. While this type of memorial may imply a certain sort of obsessiveness, it also provides some fascinating insights into the tastes and interests of a prosperous, close-knit bourgeois family in mid-nineteenth-century Paris.

Moreau's bedroom is furnished with his parents' Empire furniture, including one of their twin beds (the

THIS EXTRAORDINARY WOODEN AND GLASS
CUBE-LIKE PIECE OF FURNITURE
REVEALS 123 SMALL WORKS BY MOREAU,
INCLUDING PAINTINGS, WATERCOLORS,
AND DRAWINGS.

GUSTAVE MOREAU'S BEDROOM
IS FILLED WITH FAMILY
HEIRLOOMS, JUST AS HE LEFT IT
FOR POSTERITY.

very bed in which Moreau died), and it is painstakingly decorated with a dizzying profusion of sculptures, paintings, drawings, photographs, and bibelots of the artist and his family. The prominent display of the embroidered ceremonial jacket that Moreau wore as a member of the Institut de France—an honor bestowed upon him in 1888—reveals a touch of elitist pride.

The artist's predilection for hoarding and displaying minutiae is evident in the large glass display case hung on one wall that contains such small mementos as a pair of scissors, a magnifying glass, medals, a small portrait of his sister Camille that he drew as a child, as well as photographs of his parents, his closest friends, and himself.

Adjacent to his bedroom is the boudoir that the artist referred to as the "room that is all laid out with keepsakes from A"—fussily decorated and furnished with a yellow-silk brocade sofa and chairs that once belonged to the painter's pupil and mistress, Alexandrine Dureux. The walls of this room are hung with a

number of Moreau's paintings, water-colors, and drawings. It is presumed that Alexandrine's possessions were given to Moreau after her death in 1890.

The dimly lit corridor leading to these two rooms, whose walls are covered with drawings, paintings, and engravings by such artists as Rembrandt, Poussin, Fromentin, and Chassériau, as well as reproductions of works by Titian, Rembrandt, and Burne-Jones, was designed to show the artists whose work Moreau most admired.

From this corridor, visitors can see the garnet-colored family dining room, notable for its credenza filled with French and Italian antique ceramics, and its engravings of works by Raphael and Chassériau. Still, most of the wall space is allocated to engravings of those works that had brought Moreau success between 1864 and 1878: *Oedipus, Jason, The*

Young Man and Death, Orpheus, Sappho, The Chimera, Venus Stepping out of the Wave, and *King David.*

Although Moreau prepared his museum with care, undertaking large-scale versions of a number of his works for eventual display, preparing commentaries of major paintings and organizing his drawings, he died before he was able to oversee the hanging of his works. This mammoth task was undertaken by his old friend and chief legatee, Henri Rupp, who accomplished it within a matter of weeks. The museum was opened to the public in January 1903, with the artist Georges Rouault as curator.

Looking at Moreau's dense and baroque canvases, many of which are littered with strange and mythological apparitions, including sphinxes, griffons, centaurs, unicorns, and angels, it is difficult to believe that he worked during the same epoch as Courbet, Monet, Manet, and Renoir,

ALEXANDRINE DUREUX'S BOUDOIR,
DECORATED WITH THE
PAINTINGS THAT MOREAU HAD
GIVEN HER OVER THE YEARS.

whose chosen subjects emerged from the everyday world. In Moreau's universe, naked heroes and damsels with long flowing hair coexist with sensuous white swans and red-winged horses, as in *Hesiod and the Muses*, dally with unicorns, as in *The Unicorns*, and do battle with the pretenders to Ulysses' throne, as in *The Dissemblers*. Any visitor who has been exposed to the psychedelic art of the 1960s and 1970s will be struck by its affinity to some of Moreau's paintings.

Although the museum's presentation doesn't follow any particular chronological order (which would be difficult to establish in any case, since Moreau was constantly refinishing and embellishing his works) the third- and fourth-floor ateliers demonstrate the artist's variety and complexity. While his large-scale paintings from the years 1860–70 still tend toward academicism, his mature work, executed between 1875 and 1889, is striking for its broad and vivid brushstrokes of color and its richly decorative linear drawing. These later works, many of them brilliantly colored, exude a dreamy symbolism that captivated such Symbolists as Odilon Redon and Puvis de Chavannes, and such Surrealists as Salvador Dalí and André Breton.

Moreau's watercolors offer a lovely coherence and delicate approach quite different from that evident in the flamboyant large-scale paintings. These works are often based on mythological subjects (*Hercules and the Hydra, Apollo and Pegasus, Jason and Medea*), as well as on such biblical stories as *Moses and the Burning Bush* and *The Descent from the Cross*.

"What many people don't realize is that there are two Moreaus in this museum," notes curator Geneviève Lacambre. "One who did the showy work for clients such as Léopold Goldschmidt (who bequeathed *Jupiter and Semele* to the museum in 1903) and the one who did watercolors for himself, which are both lighter in technique and much deeper.

"Because of the Impressionists' popularity, Moreau's work has never received the attention it deserves," Lacambre points out. "Many people don't realize that it was Moreau and Symbolist painting that led the way to Surrealism."

After shunning the art world's criticism while he was alive, Moreau clearly wanted to display the achievement of a lifetime, albeit with all of its experiments and trials, triumphs and defeats, in this most personal of museums. Shortly before his death, the painter told his friend Henri Rupp: "If I have expressed in my works something that deserves to live, it will live on despite everything; if I deluded myself, the work will disappear to where all mediocre things go. I have found in the passionate cultivation of my art and in strenuous work, inexpressible pleasures: I have my reward, I ask for nothing." The Gustave Moreau Museum permits visitors to partake in that reward as well.

Le Musée Nissim de Camondo

The Nissim de Camondo Museum

63, Rue de Monceau
75008 Paris
Tel: (01) 53–89–06–40

Open every day except Monday,
Tuesday, and holidays from
10:00 A.M. to Noon and from
2:00 P.M. to 5:00 P.M.

Metro: Monceau, Villiers
Bus: 84, 94

THERE ARE at least two buildings with the architectural leitmotif of the Petit Trianon in the Paris area: the original manor is, as generally known, at Versailles, the other occupies a site on an elegant residential street adjacent to the enchanting Parc Monceau.

While Louis XVI commissioned Jacques-Ange Gabriel to build the original residence in 1763, the Parisian replica was erected between 1911 and 1914. As was true of the Queen's favorite residence at Versailles, this townhouse is sumptuously appointed with the finest in eighteenth-century tapestries, furnishings, paintings, porcelains, and bibelots.

THE FAÇADE OF
THE NISSIM DE CAMONDO MUSEUM
WAS INSPIRED BY THE
PETIT TRIANON AT VERSAILLES.

THE COLOR OF THE YELLOW SILK
WALL COVERING AND DOUBLE CURTAINS
IN THE BLUE SALON
IS REFERRED TO AS "THE QUEEN'S HAIR."

THE *SALON HUET* IS NAMED AFTER
THE FAMOUS SERIES OF PAINTINGS
BY JEAN-BAPTISTE HUET,
DEPICTING AN ARCADIAN ROMANCE.

Ironically, just as the Queen and her family suffered a tragic fate, so did the former occupants of this stately mansion, now known as the Nissim de Camondo Museum. Entering through the arched entrance that leads up to the imposing facade, one's attention is immediately caught by two marble plaques recapitulating the demise of the family's last descendants. The first plaque explains that this museum was willed to the Musée des Arts Décoratifs in Paris in 1933 by its owner, Moïse de Camondo, in memory of his son Nissim de Camondo, a lieutenant aviator who was killed in aerial combat in 1917.

The second states: "Madame Léon Reinach, born Béatrice de Camondo, and her two children, Fanny and Bertrand Reinach, the last descendants of the benefactor, and M. Léon Reinach were deported by the Germans in 1943–44 and died in Auschwitz."

Walking through the mansion's exquisitely appointed rooms, with their harmonious interrelation of *boiseries*, richly colored tapestries, sumptuous silk brocade draperies and upholstery, and paintings by Elisabeth Vigée-Lebrun and Francesco Guardi, it's understandable that connoisseurs have compared the Nissim de Camondo Museum with The Frick Collection in New York City.

The museum's extensive collections of rare hand-painted Sèvres, Meissen, and Chantilly services in the *Cabinet des Porcelaines*, its dazzling chandelier resplendent with goose-egg-size drops of amethyst, rock crystal, and smoky quartz, its still-lifes in petit-point that bear a startling resemblance to the works by Jean-Baptiste-Siméon Chardin—and these are only a smattering of the splendors on display—make an impression that can be almost overwhelming. No wonder so many antiques specialists claim that the French decorative arts reached their apex in the eighteenth century.

This museum represents the life-long passion of a collector who fell in love with the eighteenth century: Moïse de Camondo. Born in Constantinople in 1860, he spent the better part of his childhood there, until his father Nissim and his uncle Abraham Behor decided that the family's fortunes would benefit by transferring the family and its business interests to Paris.

However, it was Moïse's great-grandfather, Abraham Solomon, who exerted the greatest influence over the family's fortunes. A devout Sephardic Jew, Abraham Solomon was also a worldly one. As head of the family bank, it was he who had initially encouraged his grandsons to open a branch office of their bank, I. Camondo & Compagnie, in Paris.

OVER THE EIGHTEENTH-CENTURY
STEEL AND GILT BRONZE BED OF NISSIM DE CAMONDO
(1892–1917) IS A PORTRAIT OF HIS GRANDFATHER
BY CAROLUS-DURAN.

Although Austrian by nationality, his
affinities were Italian. In 1865, to the
great surprise of the inhabitants of
Constantinople, he and his family
obtained Italian citizenship, and
moved to Italy. He offered his financial assistance to Victor Emmanuel II
who, to express his thanks, made
Abraham Solomon a count by decree
on April 27, 1867, a title that
was transmissible through male heirs.

The exceptional qualities of
Abraham Solomon made a lasting
impression on his grandsons, Nissim
and Abraham Behor. It was on his
advice that both men acquired property on the Monceau plain. While
Abraham Behor purchased land located at number 61 on the Rue de
Monceau where he eventually built a
townhouse, Nissim acquired the
Hôtel Violet, located at number 63
Rue de Monceau (the present site of
the Nissim de Camondo Museum).

such Impressionists as Manet, Pissarro, Sisley, Monet, and Degas), Moïse limited his passion to the eighteenth century. Upon his mother's death in 1910, he inherited the family townhouse at 63 Rue de Monceau. He demolished it at the end of the year, in order to replace it with a Petit Trianon–inspired edifice built by René Sergent. The plan Sergent devised for the interior decoration was subject to various imperatives, including the antique wainscoting that Moïse had purchased for various rooms.

The museum's most impressive rooms are on the second floor. The *Grand Salon* with its gold and white wainscoting taken from a Parisian mansion on the Rue Royale, contains chairs by Jacob (Louis XVI's furniture maker) upholstered with Aubusson tapestries, and a brilliantly colored wool tapestry screen after cartoons by Alexandre-François Desportes, surprisingly unfaded. Not to be overlooked are two rare and charming end tables by Martin Carlin decorated with plaques of hand-painted Sèvres porcelain and a rather incongruous worn leather desk armchair that once belonged to the Comte d'Artois, the King's brother.

The *Salon Huet*, named after the famous series of paintings by Jean-Baptiste Huet depicting an arcadian romance, contains an exquisite wood inlay desk that, at one time, had been among the Queen's possessions, a silk brocade screen from the game-room at Versailles, a pair of silver and bronze metal consoles, as well as a tiny but impressive end-table *(table en cabaret)* made of oak and limewood and coated with a varnish in the same pattern as the table's soft-paste porcelain top.

The dining room, which overlooks a French formal garden, is notable for its watercolor green eighteenth-

The two brothers, known as "the Rothschilds of the East" kept pace with the worlds of art and finance in Paris, giving frequent receptions in their luxurious homes. Upon their deaths in 1889, they left a prosperous bank behind them. Although Abraham Behor's son Isaac took over the bank's direction in 1894, he was forced to close down the Constantinople branch due to ill health. By the time Isaac died in 1911, Moïse was no more than an administrator. When his only son, Nissim, was killed, the bank of I. Camondo & Compagnie closed permanently.

Unlike his cousin, who was eclectic in his tastes (Isaac's collections, which were bequeathed to the French state upon his death, ranged from eighteenth-century furniture to

century wainscoting, in the same tonality as the hand-painted Sèvres porcelain service on display. The warm green walls and tapestries in the room are a perfect backdrop for the massive silver tureens, ice-buckets, and other serving pieces that Catherine the Great had once ordered for her lover, the Count Orloff.

By the time Moïse took up residence with his two children, Nissim and Béatrice (his marriage to Irène Cahen d'Anvers was short-lived and ended in divorce in 1901), World War I had begun. It was to destroy the unclouded, well-ordered universe that he had worked so hard to establish. The most severe blow was the death of Nissim, who was to have inherited both the bank and this splendid home. A poignant letter of condolence from Marcel Proust, now on display in the museum, reads in part: "I cannot know whether my name will mean anything to you. I once dined with you at Madame Cahen's and more recently, though it also seems extremely remote, you took me to dine with dear Charles Ephrussi of whom I was extremely fond. All these memories appear so distant now."

Though the gods were cruel to Moïse de Camondo, they spared him the horror of seeing his only surviving child, Béatrice, arrested by the Gestapo in 1943 and deported to Auschwitz in 1944, along with her husband and two children. It seems that—despite all the signs of rampant anti-Semitism in France— Béatrice, a passionate horsewoman, continued to ride in the Bois de Boulogne with Nazi officers. After reportedly trouncing a Nazi officer in an equestrian competition at Chantilly, she was arrested and sent to Drancy, where she languished for a year before being sent to Auschwitz.

"What struck me more than anything is that this family, which had been so generous toward France, was forgotten," notes Sophie Le Tarnec, the museum's archivist, who has painstakingly uncovered much of the family's buried history. To the Vichy regime it didn't matter that Nissim de Camondo had fought for France in the previous war and had been awarded the Légion d'Honneur posthumously in 1920. Nor did it take notice of the fact that both Moïse and Isaac de Camondo had once been publicly acclaimed for their princely donations of art to the Louvre, the Musée des Arts Décoratifs, and the Musée Guimet.

In his testament, Moïse de Camondo wrote: "In bequeathing my townhouse and collections to the State, my purpose is to preserve . . . the reconstitution of a dwelling of the eighteenth century. This reconstitution is intended. . . to preserve in France . . . the finest examples I have been able to assemble of this decorative art which was one of the glories of France."

The Nissim de Camondo Museum demonstrates that, in the end, the final gift of this extraordinary collector has become part of the heritage of France and is being faithfully and splendidly perpetuated.

Le Musée de l'Outil
The Museum of Tools

Wy-dit-Joli-Village
95420 Val d'Oise
Tel: (01) 34–67–41–79

**Open to individual visitors on
Sunday afternoons from 2:30 P.M.
to 6 P.M. Open to groups by prior
appointment, Monday through
Saturday from 9:00 A.M. to Noon
and from 2:00 P.M. to 6:00 P.M.**

• **Access:**
**By car: Fifty kilometers from
La Défense, taking the direction
Cergy-Pontoise, then the N 14
toward Rouen, turn left at the
signs reading "Musée de l'Outil de
Wy" and drive three kilometers
to the museum, next to the Church
of Wy-dit-Joli-Village.**

Note:
Wy is the modern form of the Latin
word *vicus* (village). According to
local legend, when King Henry IV's
carriage got stuck in the mud on his
way to see his mistress Gabrielle
d'Estrées (1571–1599), he exclaimed
ironically: *"Quel joli village!"* (What a
pretty village!). The *dit*, meaning
"said," was added later.

MOST PEOPLE who decide
to restore their grandmother's
property don't expect to discover a
Gallo-Roman bath from the second
century A.D. beneath its foundations.
Yet, that is precisely what happened
to Claude Pigeard, while he was
preparing the premises as a setting
within which to display his extensive
collection of antique tools.

After ten years of careful digging
four meters below ground (with the
help of a team from the Center of
Archeology of Guéry-en-Vexin), he
was able to reconstruct a remarkable
spa, buried beneath sixteen centuries
of rubble, steps away from the house

THROUGH THE DOORWAY
CAN BE SEEN THE
RECONSTRUCTED FURNACE THAT
ONCE HEATED ROMAN BATHS,
BUILT IN THE SECOND CENTURY A.D.

ALL SORTS OF ARTISANAL TOOLS
FOR MAKING NAILS ARE ON DISPLAY
AT THE MUSEUM OF TOOLS.

where he was born, and next door to the one where he now resides with his wife. After excavating four meters of dirt, the team found a Roman bathers' waiting room, a *caldarium* (a hot water tub heated by an underground heating system known as a hypocaust), a *tepidarium* (a tub with warm water), and a *frigidarium* for cold baths. In 1984, the Vexin site was declared a national historic monument by the French government. Today, the excavated Roman baths are being used to display the collections of the Museum of Tools, a museum that claims to have the largest number of antique agrarian and craftsmen's implements in

Western Europe dating back to the fourteenth century. (Although only 3,500 tools are on display, the museum's holdings exceed 15,000.)

By displaying such agricultural and artisanal tools from pre-industrial France in this ancient Roman facility, the museum has become imbued with an aura of mystery and poignancy lacking in many modern institutions. The rough and simple ancient walls and floors of this atypical museum accentuate the particularity, simplicity, and beauty of each tool. Not merely the past has been unearthed at the Museum of Tools, but also the labor of generations of French peasants and craftsmen.

THE HUTCH IN THIS
EIGHTEENTH-CENTURY VEXIN KITCHEN
IS FILLED WITH
MARTINCAMP POTTERY.

"I want this museum to be a place dedicated to memory," explains Pigeard, a former assembly-line worker at Renault. "I felt these occupations were about to disappear and I wanted to keep a record of them."

Pigeard, one of the few blacksmiths left in the region, has devoted the first room in the museum to the smithy, displaying one-sided and two-sided anvils, some of which are initialed and decorated with ornate designs. Two are girthed with a farrier's tool belt, containing implements few people recognize, such as shoeing hammers, farrier's pincers, fly whisks, and horse-tail cutters. Pigeard's sheet-iron portrayal of Saint Eloi, the blacksmith's patron saint, graces one wall; opposite is a "bouquet of Saint Eloi," a late-nineteenth-century sign hung with different types of horseshoes and surrounded by a series of corrective irons that the smithy once used.

In the second room, where Pigeard has reconstructed a crescent-shaped Roman tub on the ancient foundations, tools used in farming and in the wood trades occupy the place of honor. There can be found the tools of the wheelwright, who used to make and repair the wooden wheels of carts and carriages. On one wall are all sorts of tools for cutting, digging, and planting: axes of all sizes and shapes, scythes, flails, hemp-cutters, hoes, spades, shovels, and tools for barking. There are also wolf-traps and special jugs for drinking in the fields. The arduous manual endeavors of sowing and harvesting, of sawing and chopping, of shaping logs into wheels, barrels, and wooden shoes, are eloquently conveyed through each display.

The last room pays homage to local and regional crafts and traditions. One of the most charming displays is a sprightly row of sixteenth- to nineteenth-century cast-iron wafer

THESE SICKLES AND HOES ARE AMONG THE ANTIQUE FARM IMPLEMENTS ON DISPLAY INSIDE THE FORMER GALLO-ROMAN BATH AT THE MUSEUM OF TOOLS.

molds, decorated with religious and pagan patterns and motifs, as well as the dates of special holidays and marriages, for which they were intended.

In keeping with his desire to commemorate trades that have disappeared, Pigeard has devoted corners of his museum to nail-making, rope-making, and pearling (the making of glass pearls used for chapel rosaries), as well as to wagon and carriage making.

What made him amass a collection of such tools in the first place? Pigeard credits his "spiritual father," Roland Vasseur, a local schoolteacher and independent scholar who was passionate about local folk art and culture, with inspiring him to value the beauty and history of tools.

"When we met I didn't know much," he recalls. "He showed me my mistakes and helped me to learn about the houses and traditions of the

THESE OLD-FASHIONED ANVILS
WERE ONCE USED
TO MAKE KEYS SUCH AS THOSE
SHOWN IN THE FRAME.

THIS EXHIBIT OF WOOD, TOOLS,
AND SHOES IS INTENDED
TO CONVEY HOW WOODEN SHOES
WERE ONCE MADE.

Vexin. I would bring him tools and objects I didn't recognize and he would identify them for me, explaining their uses, which had often been forgotten. Most of what I know I learned through him."

Not content with showing tools in the context of a former Gallo-Roman bath, two years ago Pigeard decided to recreate the atmosphere of an eighteenth-century home in rural France within two rooms of his house, and open them up to visitors. Next to his modern Provençal-style kitchen, he recreated a traditional eighteenth-century beamed Vexin kitchen with a plaster fireplace, outfitted with a hand-held rotisserie. The antique table, benches, and kitchen hutch filled with bright yellow Martincamp earthenware from nearby Forge-les-Eaux, were once typical furnishings of rural homes in this area.

A prototype rustic bedroom is furnished with an oxblood-colored eighteenth-century canopy bed and matching rectangular table. "These pieces were made on the Guérande peninsula in Brittany, near Nantes," Pigeard explains. "The idea for painting the furniture red came from sailors who had been to China. Tradition has it that they were repainted at Easter to commemorate the blood of Christ."

Besides protecting the fleeting heritage of French rural life, the Museum of Tools has also recreated one of the loveliest medieval presbytery gardens in France. Bordered with boxwood, this garden is separated into smaller units serving different functions: a variegated cutting garden for altar bouquets planted with annuals such as daisies, zinnias, cosmoses, snapdragons, and rockets; a kitchen garden with miniature pear and apple trees, potatoes, radishes, peas, pumpkins, raspberry, strawberry, and gooseberry

THIS OXBLOOD-RED LOUIS XIII-STYLE FURNITURE
WAS ONCE IN THE HOME OF
AN EIGHTEENTH-CENTURY SALT-SELLER ON THE
GUÉRANDE PENINSULA NEAR NANTES.

plants; a medicinal garden with herbal plants such as tansy and rue (the latter, used in primitive abortions, was often deadly); an herb garden that boasts fifteen varieties of mint, as well as herbal tea plants; and a rose garden, featuring roses brought back from the Crusades in the thirteenth century.

The same love of detail and craftsmanship that characterizes the museum's tool displays, is also evident in this enchanting historic garden. The wooden posts supporting plants and vines are painted blue to ward off flies and bugs, a practice that began in the Middle Ages. Each plant is tagged with a hand-tooled sign made of sheet-iron. Propped in a corner of the garden beneath some bushes is a hand-engraved sheet-iron facsimile of Jean de La Fontaine's poem *The Laborer and His Children*. The fable's moral reads: *Mais le Père fut sage/De leur montrer avant sa mort/Que le travail est un trésor.* (But the father was wise / To show his sons before he died / That work was a treasure.)

Claude Pigeard can also be likened to a "wise father" in striving to pass on the folklore and beauty of tools and trades in his highly evocative rural museum. In championing these lost or forgotten "treasures," his Museum of Tools causes us to consider that some of the most remarkable things come out of the ground we walk on and often take for granted—be they roses brought back from the Crusades, or a Gallo-Roman bath hidden in the ground for centuries.

Le Musée Edith Piaf

The Edith Piaf Museum

5, Rue Crespin du Gast
75011 Paris
Tel: (01) 43–55–52–72

Visits by appointment only,
Monday through Thursday from
1:00 P.M. to 6:00 P.M.

Metro: Ménilmontant, Saint-Maur
Bus: 46, 61, 69, 96

AN ASSEMBLY OF IMAGES
OF EDITH PIAF,
INCLUDING A SCULPTURE
BY MADELEINE MONNOT,
AT THE EDITH PIAF MUSEUM.

FEW PEOPLE know that hidden behind an unassuming limestone building in Ménilmontant, is the Edith Piaf Museum, only blocks away from the very streets where "the Little Sparrow" first sang, and the Père Lachaise Cemetery where she now lies buried. Although it is rarely publicized, fans avid to know more about the woman whose haunting voice sent shivers down the spine of the world, make their way to 5, Rue Crespin du Gast, where they press the four-digit code that will allow them to enter the building, and brave the climb up four flights of sheet-vinyl-covered stairs to two tiny rooms brimming over with the singer's records, memorabilia, and personal possessions. (This hard-to-find museum is among the few in Paris where visitors need to make an appointment to gain access.)

Visitors are greeted at the door by the museum's curator, Bernard Marchois, who has set aside two rooms in his apartment to create the museum, and who willingly answers any questions about the French singer's life and career. At his heels is Nankin, his Pekingese dog, who eyes each new arrival warily, acting as if he is the self-appointed guardian of the Piaf legacy.

But even if one has to confront this dog's vigilant stare, it is only here that one will be able to see and touch Piaf's unforgettable black stage dress with its sweetheart neckline, the delicate gold cross that never left her neck, and the tiny, handmade, size four shoes she wore. "Her stage dress is what touches people most," notes Marchois. "It is very, very symbolic.

One can't conceive of Piaf wearing another dress. It's like Charlie Chaplin's cane or Maurice Chevalier's straw hat."

A black-and-white life-size photograph stuck on a cardboard silhouette of Piaf singing shows that this international powerhouse entertainer stood about four-and-a-half-feet tall, not much bigger than her favorite giant stuffed bear, which stands guard nearby. That this poignant, unforgettable talent influenced countless artists and writers throughout the world is much in evidence on the apartment's walls, crammed as they are with paintings, cartoons, photographs, letters, and tributes from such admirers as actors Jean Marais, Jean-Louis Barrault, and the entertainer Maurice Chevalier. Listening to her unique rendition of such titles as *La Vie en Rose* (a song she wrote), *Milord* and *La Foule* on the museum's stereo system only confirms Barrault's handwritten tribute: "Everything she did or sang, touched the heart."

Although Edith Piaf is said to have sold more records than any other singer in history, by 1967 (four years after her death), friends and family close to her began to worry that the media were neglecting her and diminishing her importance. This concern prompted Piaf's brother and sister, Denise and Herbert Gassion, to establish "The Friends of Edith Piaf" association, which now has over 6,000 members worldwide. A decade later the association opened the Edith Piaf Museum, to show the singer's few remaining personal effects taken from her apartment in Paris, along with the many portraits and other assorted memorabilia associated with her, in the eventuality that they ultimately may be bequeathed to the as-yet-unbuilt *Musée de la Chanson Française* (Museum of French Song).

Unlike most curators, Marchois enjoyed a privileged relationship with the museum's principal subject. He was only sixteen when he was first personally introduced to Piaf, and ruefully recalls how he was initially reluctant to see her. "I was a fan of the English Teddy Boys, and had never heard of Piaf," he says. "I told my parents that I had no desire to meet her. 'You're going to go,' they insisted. 'She is a great singer.'

"We first met in her huge apartment on the Boulevard Lanne during one of her rehearsals. I was sitting on the same blue velvet banquette that you now see here. It was about two o'clock in the afternoon.

"Out came this woman in a dressing gown such as you see here, only it was blue instead of red, like this one," he continues, pointing to the modest

EDITH PIAF'S
EVER SO PETITE BLACK DRESS
STANDS NEAR HER
STUFFED BEAR AND MONKEY,
WHICH ACCOMPANIED HER
EVERYWHERE FOR GOOD LUCK.

cerise velvet peignoir on a dress-maker's dummy, next to an antique oak armoire that also once belonged to Piaf.

"She wore a kerchief on her head and had some grease on her lips. She didn't even have her hair combed. 'These adults are completely crazy. This isn't a great singer. She isn't even beautiful,' I thought to myself. Then I heard her sing. It's amazing to think that I almost dismissed who she was. I ended up asking her permission to watch her backstage for the next three months while she filled the Olympia every night, something I am so grateful she let me do."

Today, Marchois is not only the museum's curator, but an author who has spent the last quarter-century preparing a prize-winning book published in 1993, *Piaf Emportée par la Foule* (*Piaf Carried Away by the Crowd*), which includes photographs never seen before, as well as a detailed daily agenda of the singer's personal and professional life.

The most striking aspects of the museum are the numerous portraits, sculptures, and drawings of Piaf exhibiting every conceivable expression: unbridled joy, world-weary irony, implacable sorrow, and contemplative serenity. Withal, her unique magnetism and fiery personality are apparent, no matter how she is portrayed. Perhaps the most arresting portraits are those by Charles Kieffer, often called the "twentieth century's Toulouse-Lautrec," who created Piaf's first concert poster in 1937 (also on view).

Visitors who take the time to talk to Marchois may uncover some surprising facts about Piaf. "While many people were eager to reproach Piaf for singing during the war, most didn't realize that she was forced by the Germans to do so," notes Marchois. "What they also don't know is that it was through her singing in Germany that she was able to help over 100 prisoners escape."

A COUCH AND ARMOIRE FROM PIAF'S APARTMENT ON THE RUE LANNE, A DRESSING GOWN OF RED VELVET THAT SHE USED TO WEAR DURING HER REHEARSALS, AND SOME OF HER GOLD AND PLATINUM RECORDS ARE SHOWN HERE.

THIS BOOKCASE IS FILLED WITH
PIAF MEMORABILIA,
INCLUDING HER CROCODILE POCKETBOOK.

Marchois recounts that when Piaf was on one of her concert tours, she would make sure to be photographed with the French prisoners. Back in Paris, she had the photos enlarged, cut out and inserted into false identity cards that later enabled these same prisoners to escape. Pulling a small faded and frayed French flag from a black crocodile handbag formerly carried by the singer, Marchois tells how this flag was given to Piaf by French former prisoners of war in homage and gratitude for her vital assistance.

"Visitors like the intimate side of this museum," observes Marchois. "One often has the impression that Piaf herself is going to emerge at any moment from behind the door. In fact, one woman who came here, who was a medium, told me that she had goosebumps, because she felt Piaf's very presence.

" 'I feel it, Piaf lives here,' she told me. 'You have a plan to put her somewhere else, but you will have a hard time doing so.' Well, for over ten years we have been trying to open the *Musée de la Chanson Francaise*, and we haven't made much progress. It seems that she wants to stay here." In the meantime, she still has many long-standing admirers happy to visit her and keep her company in the intimate precincts of the Edith Piaf Museum.

Le Musée de la Poupée
The Doll Museum

Impasse Berthaud
75003 Paris
Tel: (01) 42–72–73–11

Open Wednesday through Sunday
from 10:00 A.M. to 1:00 P.M.
and from 2:00 P.M. to 6:30 P.M.;
Thursday evenings from
8:00 P.M. to 10:30 P.M.

Metro: Rambuteau
Bus: 21, 29, 38, 47, 58

THE ENTRANCE TO THE DOLL MUSEUM,
OFF A NARROW PASSAGE
IN THE MARAIS, IS FILLED WITH VINES
AND FLOWERS IN THE SUMMER.

THROUGH THE WOOD-FRAMED
ARCHWAY AT THE DOLL MUSEUM
ARE ROWS OF GLASS CASES
DISPLAYING RARE FRENCH DOLLS.

IF THERE IS a single word that aptly describes the *Musée de la Poupée* (The Doll Museum), it is: enchanting. Hidden behind one of those narrow dead-end streets known as *passages*, so characteristic of Paris, is the city's only museum dedicated to the collection and permanent display of French unglazed hand-painted porcelain dolls, most of which were manufactured between 1860 and 1960 (when the popularity of such dolls was at its zenith). Connoisseurs and collectors will recognize and appreciate the exceptional craftsmanship epitomized by the museum's collection of *bébés* whether they represent dolls by Schmitt, Steiner, Gaultier, Halopeau, Thuillier, Bru, or Jumeau—all nineteenth-century household names to the families of the aristocracy and the well-to-do. Today, these dolls have become prized rarities and many are considered works of art.

The Doll Museum, which opened in June 1994, is all the more unusual because the 200 dolls on permanent display behind glass are dramatically presented in a series of imaginary vignettes intended to captivate visitors of all ages. One doesn't need to be a doll collector to love this museum. It's easy to be drawn into the miniature presentations of dolls playing in the nursery with toys from the period, dolls at the beach, dolls selling cotton goods and sewing notions, as well as dolls out for a stroll in the park.

Their expressions are equally fascinating. There are dolls staring dreamily into their wardrobe mirrors as they try on opulent silk gowns, a

doll demurely serving other dolls tea, a doll with a dunce cap on its head, seated ashamedly before its school-mates, and a family of dolls playing with puppets and puzzles and wooden blocks. And this is only a sampling of the forty-two tableaux of genteel domesticity that will transport any visitor from the everyday world to a wonderful lilliputian universe where all things seem possible, and where a nanny such as Mary Poppins would feel right at home.

"We wanted to present the dolls in specific settings in a period decor scaled to the dolls' height," explains Samy Odin, co-director and co-founder of the museum. "We felt that if we didn't show the dolls with these backdrops, we would deny the museum the imaginative riches of children and their games."

Samy Odin's fascination with dolls —a passion he shares with his father, Guido—began by happenstance fifteen years ago, when he was a six-teen-year-old teenager living in Torre Pellice, a small town near Turin in Northern Italy. "My father gave me an old porcelain doll that a woman in the town had given to him, knowing that he collected antiques," he recalls. "Seeing that I was curious about the doll's origins, he then gave me a book on old dolls for my birthday. We tried to see if there was a doll in the book that resembled the doll I had. (There wasn't.) It was then that I began to see that dolls were very interesting from both a cultural and an aesthetic standpoint."

It wasn't long before the acquisi-tion of this first doll turned into a passion for collecting. Between 1981, when Samy Odin was given his first doll, and 1994, father and son together had amassed over 1,000 dolls, most of them French in origin. Because of the museum's limited space, only a fraction of the collection is displayed at any one time. However, many dolls kept in reserve are often shown in temporary themed exhibits, which change about every six months.

While the majority of visitors appreciate the highly imaginative settings for the dolls, the museum also appeals to knowledgeable collectors. "There are many exceptional dolls that make a special trip to this museum worthwhile for a collector," notes Odin. "For instance, we have a very rare *Bébé Halopeau* (a doll made by M. Halopeau between 1882 and 1888; the only other example of such a doll in a European museum is at the Puppen Museum in Stein um Rhien in Switzerland).

"We also have a very rare *Bébé Thuillier,* one of the finest porcelain dolls ever produced, which is particularly coveted by collectors because of its sweet and tearful expression."

The museum has a wonderful collection of *Parisiennes*—also known as "dolls of fashion"—which were used by dressmakers and couturiers before fashion illustration came into vogue. These dolls provide a good idea of mid-nineteenth-century standards of beauty: pale skin, smooth features, and a solid, curvaceous build. (Barbie would be introduced only a good hundred years later.) While these dolls have fetching pink cheeks and tiny pursed rosebud mouths, they also exude a certain imperiousness: their glass eyes stare fixedly into space under raised eyebrows conveying a touch of haughtiness. (Although the museum has a number of dolls with moving parts, most of these dolls' lips are tightly sealed, an aesthetic preference during the classic period of their production.)

Class distinctions even among dolls are evident at this museum. For instance, in a vignette titled *"Le Marché" ("The Market")* the elegantly dressed adult dolls and child dolls contrast sharply with the roughly dressed dolls selling flowers, fruits and pottery. In another titled *"Madame! Votre Ombrelle!" ("Madame! Your Parasol!")* the vitrine shows a pair of fashionably dressed, lifelike dolls setting out for a stroll, while their parlor maid bashfully proffers a leather umbrella.

Most of the museum's permanent collection consists of *bébés* however— two to three-foot-high porcelain dolls in the very image of the nineteenth-century children who owned them. "While the 1860s and 1870s were the golden age of the *Parisiennes,*" says Odin, "by 1878 manufacturers like Jumeau, Petit & Dumoutier, and Steiner had begun to manufacture porcelain dolls that resembled young children, which are known as *bébés*. This development reflected a profound change in thinking: it seemed that children preferred a doll in their own image, compared with the adult model to which they were expected to aspire."

The most poignant of the museum's vignettes, titled *"Quelle Triste Malheur" ("What A Sad Misfortune!")* shows a taffeta-clad doll (Cody Jumeau) standing stricken before a brass inlaid fireplace, stunned by the sight of her own doll with its skull cracked open.

"We wanted to show a scene that would help explain why so few of these porcelain dolls have survived to this day," notes Odin. "Moreover, by showing the crushed doll, we were also able to show how it was made.

"The intent of this museum is to address the public on several levels," he adds. "Through our displays we want people to know more about the culture and customs of the period, about games that no longer exist, such as the magic lantern, or certain block games.

"In order to understand this museum, you have to see that it is about the naive and poetic world of children. We also want to show how the development of the porcelain doll was an outgrowth of industrialization.

"At the same time, the number of different dolls from the same period demonstrates the growth in industrialization and competition," he continues. "Each of these manufacturers was busy trying to outdo the other, in order to capture the child's interest. The nineteenth century, particularly the end of it, was the beginning of manufacturers marketing specifically toward children."

The growth of the doll market expanded significantly under the Third Republic, as the standard of living of the French *petit bourgeois* improved. Dolls that had once been reserved only for the children of the wealthy could now be purchased by middle and even the lower class families for their children. In 1878 Jumeau, one of the leading manufacturers, had sold 10,000 dolls; twenty years later he was producing and selling three million. Still, despite the considerable technical progress made in France in the doll manufacturing sector, the cost of labor and, consequently, the price of the finished product were much higher than in Germany. Not only did small factories have difficulty competing, but even big firms such as Bru, Gaultier, and Jumeau were unable to resist the onslaught of German competition.

By the end of the nineteenth century, the golden age of the *bébé français* had peaked and French porcelain dolls had become an endangered species, rapidly being

"LA ROBE DES RÊVES"
("THE DRESS OF HER DREAMS"):
THIS *BÉBÉ BRU* WITH HER
MOVEABLE HEAD, PURSED MOUTH AND
FIXED ENAMEL EYES,
HAS ALL THE ATTRIBUTES OF
A FRENCH COQUETTE. 1885-89.
(PHOTO BY GUIDO ODIN,
MUSÉE DE LA POUPÉE, PARIS.)

replaced by their German rivals.

Both Guido and Samy Odin believe that a visit to the Doll Museum satisfies a certain desire in people to see a likeness of themselves that is situated firmly in the field of art.

"The doll corresponds to a fundamental cultural need," Samy Odin explains. "This object has been present in all civilizations and, in many instances, has been regarded as a work of art. It's precisely this historical interest, as well as its aesthetic attributes, that have accorded the doll its rightful place in its own museum."

Le Musée Maurice Ravel

The Maurice Ravel Museum

5, Rue Maurice Ravel
78490 Montfort l'Amaury
Tel: (01) 34–86–00–89

Open Monday, Wednesday, and
Thursday from 2:30 P.M. to
5:30 P.M.; Saturday and Sunday
from 10:00 A.M. to Noon
and from 2:30 P.M. to 5:30 P.M.

Access:
- **By train: Take the train from the Gare Montparnasse, direction Dreux; get off at Montfort l'Amaury-Méré. Take the bus from the train station to Montfort l'Amaury (five-minute walk to the museum).**

- **By car: Take the Autoroute A13 from the Pont de Saint-Cloud, which goes into Autoroute A12, direction Dreux; take the exit Montfort-l'Amaury until you get to the Place de l'Eglise in Montfort-l'Amaury. Follow the signs to the "Musée Maurice Ravel."**

Fifty kilometers outside Paris, in the picturesque town of Montfort-l'Amaury, known for its winding old streets and splendid Gothic cathedral, is the lovingly preserved home of Maurice Ravel, one of the most notable composers of the twentieth century.

Once known as *Le Belvédère*, it has since been renamed the Maurice Ravel Museum. Yet, after a visit to its charmingly decorated, sun-lit rooms that still resound with the composer's music, it seems almost a misnomer to call this home a museum. Little has changed since the Basque-born composer lived here:

SHOWN HERE IS THE REAR OF THE WISTERIA-COVERED
BELVÉDÈRE WITH ITS "JAPANESE" GARDEN.
RAVEL TOOK GREAT PAINS WITH ITS ARRANGEMENT,
INSTALLING A FOUNTAIN AND MINIATURE TREES, AS WELL
AS A MINIATURE JAPANESE TEMPLE.

RAVEL'S BATHROOM DRESSING TABLE LAID OUT WITH HIS
EXTENSIVE MANICURE SET; NOTHING HAS CHANGED SINCE HE LAST USED IT.

his toothbrushes and manicure set are neatly laid out in his bathroom, ready for the morning toilette; his eyeglass case still lies atop the Hérard piano next to the Maëlzel metronome; his delicate yellow and white porcelain coffee service is ready for guests in the salon.

Ravel purchased the *Belvédère*, (named after the belfry in its roof) in April 1921, having fallen in love with the splendid view and peaceful quiet of the rolling green hills of Montfort-l'Amaury that he could see from his balcony.

Despite his taxing work schedule, Ravel took a lively interest in interior decoration and gardening, and spent many months transforming his home, tracing room plans, tearing down walls, adding a wing, and ultimately converting it from a four-room cottage into a ten-room house.

The decor reveals a man with distinct tastes. Not only did Ravel choose to paint the walls navy blue and yellow ochre—daring colors at the time—but he also conceived the designs for the rooms' wallpapers and hand-painted frieze in the dining

such works as *Tzigane, The Sonata for Violin and Piano, Two Concertos for Piano,* and *The Monégasque Songs,* is a curious blend of sobriety and whimsy: on the wall above his piano is the portrait of his formidable mother; on the facing wall, a bamboo étagère filled with assorted knick-knacks, including a miniature porcelain sofa; on his simple wooden desk, a brass inkwell shaped like a cathedral holds a goose-quill pen.

In her 1939 memoir, *Maurice Ravel as Seen by Some of His Intimates,* violinist Hélène Jourdan-Morhange recalls that Ravel liked to tease his guests by showing them into his fake Japanese salon, which remains unchanged to this day. "He would let his guests venture polite admiration for the decor, only to erupt with, 'It's fake!' His biggest stunt was a smoked crystal ball that he had mounted like a rare object on a base that he himself had painted. He would hold it carefully up to his guests who would solemnly murmur: 'It's very beautiful,' only to see their host burst into peals of laughter and exclaim: 'It's only a scorched electric bulb!'" Visitors to the museum can still see the object that caused such unexpected mirth on so many occasions.

Ravel, who spoke both French and Basque, was also a prolific and eclectic reader, as evidenced by the many beautifully bound books in his library, including works by Pascal, Spinoza, and Voltaire, along with the memoirs of Casanova, Saint-Simon, and the Prince de Ligne. This room also contains a victrola that no longer works. The only record left in the house is Ravel's own recording of the *Bolero.*

Ravel spent the most creative and productive years of his relatively short life (he died at the age of sixty-two) at Montfort-l'Amaury. It was here that he wrote the music to Colette's poetic libretto *L'Enfant et*

room, as well as the hand-stenciled columns in his bedroom. Obsessed with detail, he designed special vitrines in the living room to display his extensive collection of china and bibelots, transformed one of the display cabinets into a secret closet, and even created a decorative motif for his Louis-Philippe dining room chairs.

Ravel loved to collect all sorts of bric-à-brac and china from his friends, as well as from flea markets. Throughout the house the visitor will find displays of china figurines and teapots, colored boxes, glass trinkets, children's games, dolls, and automatons.

Even his study, where he spent arduous, sleepless nights composing

A CLOSE-UP OF THE FIREPLACE MANTEL
IN RAVEL'S BEDROOM.
ABOVE THE MIRROR IS A CHARMING
ANONYMOUS LANDSCAPE.

It seems that Ravel was delighted with the commission and the technical problems that would have to be surmounted in creating a left-hand piece. "The concerto must not be a stunt," he told Wittgenstein. "The listener must never feel that more could have been accomplished with two hands." Wittgenstein first heard the finished work at the *Belvédère* in August 1930, and was initially less than thrilled with the piece. He feared that much of the piano part, especially in the middle of the work, would be overwhelmed by the orchestra.

In his article, "The Other Wittgenstein," published in *The American Scholar*, J. F. Penrose writes: "Although Wittgenstein asked for a more prominent role for the piano, Ravel refused, insisting that it would ruin the work. After months of discussion, Wittgenstein capitulated and played the work as written. It became his signature piece and was the means by which Wittgenstein made his triumphant entry to the American concert scene in 1934."

Although the composer had hoped to find a refuge from the hectic life of concerts and commissions, criticism and controversy at his wisteria-covered country home, by 1931 he was confiding to the critic José Bruyr: "I work a lot and barely sleep two hours a night." One evening, Hélène Jourdan-Morhange, while accompanying him in his *Sonata for Piano and Violin*, found him "so strange, so lost in his music" that she confided her worry to the professor and physician Pasteur Vallery-Radot, who recommended that he rest for a year. Heeding this early warning sign, Ravel reduced his activities. Nonetheless, it was too late; the illness (later diagnosed as aphasia and apraxia) that had overtaken him continued its insidious progression.

les Sortilèges *(The Child and the Spells)*, inspired by his many nocturnal hikes in the woods of Rambouillet, where he clarified and developed ideas as they came to him. During the seven years he worked on the composition, he only met with Colette twice to discuss the piece, even though she resided in nearby Méré. "He was worried only about the duo between the two cats and asked me whether I had any problem if he replaced 'mouaô' by 'mouain' or the contrary," Colette recalls in her memoirs.

Another unusual piece that Ravel composed at the *Belvédère* was the heart-rending *Concerto in D Major*, perhaps the best-known work for the left hand, created for Paul Wittgenstein, the renowned one-armed pianist and brother of the philosopher Ludwig Wittgenstein.

THE BLACK-AND-WHITE CHECKERBOARD FLOORING,
STRIPED WALLPAPER, AND PATCHWORK PILLOWS
IN THE LIVING ROOM, WERE ALL CHOSEN BY THE COMPOSER.

In the summer of 1932, Ravel composed his final work, *Don Quixote to Dulcinea*, set to texts by Paul Morand. Following an accident in a Paris taxi in October 1932, Ravel grew worse. His body refused to perform certain movements, and his hands had become rigid. Writing had become so difficult that he was forced to abandon it. He could no longer sign his name, even for admirers requesting his autograph.

Tragically, he was denied that which he loved most: his music. Gradually, he lost his ability to read a musical score, and found it difficult even to discern the notes on his beloved keyboard. In 1937, during a festival of his works, Ravel confided to his friend Louis Aubert: "Now it's all over for me." After unsuccessful

brain surgery on December 19, 1937, the composer slipped into a coma. He died eight days later, never having regained consciousness.

Seeing the unaltered state of the *Belvédère* and its grounds, it is difficult to believe that the composer of such captivating music is no longer present. In her memoirs, Colette Loubet-Durègne writes: "The walker who wanders in the forest, who listens to its murmurs, doesn't he realize that the shadow of Maurice Ravel is present everywhere? Ravel, poet and magician, found in the forest of Rambouillet his baton which brought to life a fabulous and fanciful world: the world of *Magic Spells*." In Ravel's home at Montfort-l'Amaury the spell remains unbroken.

Le Musée National de la Renaissance
— Le Château d'Ecouen

The National Museum of the Renaissance
— The Château d'Ecouen

Château d'Ecouen
95440 Ecouen
Tel: (01) 39–90–04–04

Open every day except Tuesday from 9:45 A.M. to 12:30 P.M. and from 2:00 P.M. to 5:15 P.M.

Access:
- **By train: Take the train to Ecouen-Ezanville from the Gare du Nord. At the Gare Ecouen-Ezanville, take the 269 bus that goes directly to the Château d'Ecouen.**

- **By car: Take the highway A1, exit Pierrefitte, then Nationale 16 toward Chantilly, exit Ecouen. Follow the signs indicating "Musée National de la Renaissance."**

WHEN DISCUSSING legendary châteaux of the Renaissance, those that immediately come to mind are the grand edifices built along the banks of the Loire River, such as Chenonceaux, Blois, Chambord, or Azay-le-Rideau. Not many people realize that, only twenty kilometers north of Paris, they can explore a splendid Renaissance castle, the Château d'Ecouen, built around 1538 and completed around 1555, by the Duke Anne de Montmorency, the High Constable to the Kings Francis I and Henry II. As the King's prime-minister, Montmorency was the second most powerful man in France, and one of the wealthiest. His property amounted to six hundred fiefs and one hundred and thirty châteaux scattered throughout the northern half of the kingdom.

Constructed atop a hill 150 meters high, overlooking the gold and green plains of the Ile-de-France, the classical Château d'Ecouen is now home to the National Museum of the Renaissance, which contains one of the most sumptuous and extensive collections of rare tapestries, furniture, goldsmith's work, tilework, ceramics, painted enamels, glass, and sculpture from the period.

Unlike examples of the other prestigious group of royal residences in the Ile-de-France, such as Fontainebleau, Saint-Germain-en-Laye, and Anet, which were either destroyed or modified during and after the French Revolution, Ecouen's

THE WESTERN FACADE OF THE CHATEAU D'ECOUEN,
THE ONLY RENAISSANCE CASTLE IN THE ILE-DE-FRANCE THAT WAS
STILL VIRTUALLY INTACT AFTER THE FRENCH REVOLUTION.
(COURTESY MUSÉE NATIONAL DE LA RENAISSANCE/RMN.)

monumental architecture has remained virtually intact since it was first built. The creamy white stone castle is notable for its simple and austere design: a quadrilateral structure with square pavilions on the external corners and a large courtyard in the center. A dry moat surrounds the three sides of the edifice, but is interrupted by a terrace overlooking the plain, now used as an outdoor café in the summer.

The Château was used mainly as a hunting lodge by the High Constable, Henry II, and Catherine de' Medicis. A considerate host, Montmorency built an impressive staircase for his royal guests, as well as two porticoes decorated with the King and Queen's insignia. The Slaves Portico, designed circa 1555 by Jean Bullant—one of the three greatest architects of the period—is the castle's most notable architectural feature. Embellished by four columns rising up to the eaves, it is the first known example of a Colossal order in French architecture, revealing Bullant's admiration for and knowledge of antiquity. Montmorency used it as the setting for Michelangelo's *Slaves*, a gift from Henry II (the original versions of which are now in the Louvre).

Although the High Constable was beset by the political and religious upheavals characteristic of the period, he nonetheless found time to emulate his royal masters as an ardent supporter of the arts. A man of superb taste and erudition, he helped to launch the artistic careers of a number of French artists, including the potter Masséot Abaquesne, the Protestant ceramicist Bernard Palissy, and the classically-trained architects Jean Goujon and Jean Bullant. His admiration for Roman architecture even compelled him to take steps to protect the *Maison Carrée* at Nîmes, which was being used as a quarry.

While the Château's interiors have lost a great deal of their magnificence, some of the original decor remains,

THE IMPOSING PSYCHE GALLERY, WHICH IS DECORATED WITH
ROMAN BUSTS AND SEGMENTS OF THE *DAVID AND BATHSHEBA* TAPESTRIES,
IS USED FOR CHAMBER CONCERTS DURING THE SUMMER.

particularly in the chapel and in the rooms on the second floor, thus evoking the atmosphere of a powerful lord's manor at the height of the Renaissance. The chapel has retained its vaulted ceiling embellished with the emblems of Montmorency.

Among the most innovative and impressive aspects of the Château's interior are the twelve brilliantly colored painted fireplaces located on the ground floor and the second floor, which have an identical design: a circular, oval, or rectangular frame encloses a painted scene, around which are arranged painted strapwork, fruit garlands, and *putti*. The subjects of these lively and whimsical paintings —except for *The Tribute to Caesar* which is from the Gospels—are taken from the Old Testament, including *Solomon and the Queen of Sheba* (Arms Room), *Elijah Sacrificing on Mount Carmel* (Catherine de' Medicis's bedchamber), *Esau Hunting* and *Jacob Tending Laban's Flocks*

(Montmorency's bedchamber), *Jacob Fleeing Before Laban,* and *Jacob's Arrival in the Land of Canaan.*

While the painted fireplaces are unique, the undisputed masterpiece at the Château d'Ecouen are the *David and Bathsheba* tapestries, regarded as the most important tapestry series from the early sixteenth century. These ten wall hangings, which are in superb condition, now dominate three vast rooms in the castle, reaching a total length of 250 feet with a height of over 13 feet. Woven of wool with highlights of silk, silver, and silver-gilt threads, and based on cartoons by the painter Jan Van Room (also known as Jean de Bruxelles), these exquisite and evocative hangings depict the story of David and Bathsheba's illicit love, the war waged against the Ammonites, and the siege laid before Rabbah, as well as David's repentance for sending Bathsheba's husband to his death.

Tapestry was not the only type of wall hanging favored during the Renaissance. The most unusual wall decoration at Ecouen consists of the two series of sixteenth-century painted leather wall-hangings carefully preserved in chilled rooms: the first series illustrates the *Story of Scipio*, while the second, based on engravings by Hendrik Goltzius, portrays Roman heroes. Although very fashionable until the advent of wallpaper in the eighteenth century, few of them have survived; in fact, Ecouen is the only French château to display this type of wall hanging.

Princes and great lords such as Montmorency, who had the means to commission such luxurious wall coverings, often displayed great interest in science and technology as well. One of the ground-floor rooms in the National Museum of the Renaissance displays a phenomenal collection of scientific instruments and rarities, each one a dazzling work of art. Among the noteworthy exhibits: a sundial in the form of a chalice cup, that tells the hours when it is filled with water, and a brass spherical *Map of the Heavens* made in 1502, of which only two other examples exist.

The most outstanding piece in the collection is a combination clock-automaton in the shape of a ship made circa 1580 by Hans Schlottheim of Augsburg, formerly known as the *Nef of Emperor Charles the Fifth*. When the clock was in use, the ship rolled forward on its enamel sea, the tiny musicians aboard lifted their instruments to their lips, the cannons moved, the look-outs spun in the crow's nests, while a miniature organ played as the courtiers paraded around a miniature version of an emperor seated on his throne!

This thirst to acquire the unusual, the exotic, and the exquisite, would also inspire goldsmiths to create

THIS MOTHER-OF-PEARL AND SILVER-GILT GOBLET, WITH A SNAIL MOTIF, WAS MADE IN NUREMBERG AT THE END OF THE SIXTEENTH CENTURY. (COURTESY MUSÉE NATIONAL DE LA RENAISSANCE/RMN.)

dazzling objects using ostrich eggs, nautilus shells, and coconuts that were set in silver and gold mounting and decorated with precious and semi-precious stones, some of which are displayed in a Fort Knox-like room in the Château. One of the most unusual examples of this work is the strange and exquisite *Daphne* by the Nuremberg goldsmith Wenzel Jamnitzer (1508–1585), splendidly illustrating the *recherché* style known as Mannerism, with its sinuous figure and varied materials, including silver, silver-gilt, precious and semi-precious stones, coral, and enameling.

A visit to the Château shows that even the most commonplace objects, such as keys, locks, tools, and chests, were embellished with rich carvings and paintings. Fifteenth-century Florence was famed for its *cassoni*, sumptuous bridal chests, painted with scenes drawn from ancient history or the Bible. In the eighteenth and nineteenth centuries, collectors disjoined the painted panels and displayed them as separate pictures. The museum's display of these extant panels, some of which were painted by Masaccio's brother Giovanni di Ser Giovanni, provide an excellent insight—on an

THIS MANNERIST SILVER CENTERPIECE WAS CREATED BY WENZEL JAMNITZER (1508–1585) OF NUREMBERG, ONE OF THE PERIOD'S FINEST GOLDSMITHS. (COURTESY MUSÉE NATIONAL DE LA RENAISSANCE/RMN.)

THIS CLOCK-AUTOMATON IN THE SHAPE OF A VESSEL WAS MADE BY THE AUGSBURG GOLDSMITH HANS SCHLOTTHEIM (1545–1625). (COURTESY MUSÉE NATIONAL DE LA RENAISSANCE/RMN.)

THE "ARSENAL ROOM" STILL RETAINS
A PAINTED FIREPLACE DEPICTING
A SACRIFICE BY KING SAUL OF ISRAEL.

intimate, domestic scale—into the Florentine masters of the *Quattrocento*.

The Renaissance was also a period of great innovation in the ceramic arts, and these are well-represented in the museum's collection. Ecouen boasts the third largest collection of Iznik ceramics in the world, demonstrating the noteworthy development of Ottoman art under Süleyman the Magnificent (1494–1566) and his successors. Their beautiful and intricate, predominantly blue and white floral designs, combining hyacinths, roses, and pinks on plates and tilework, evoke the great wall designs on Istanbul's mosques.

All the objects on display at the National Museum of the Renaissance, whether extraordinary or mundane, bear witness to the artistry and extreme care taken by craftsmen to satisfy their refined and demanding patrons. As was true of the former occupants, we now have the pleasure of learning more about those arts and sciences that attained new heights during this period, and that continue to move us with wonder and admiration four hundred years later.

Le Musée Erik Satie — Le Placard d'Erik Satie

The Erik Satie Museum — The Closet of Erik Satie

6, Rue Cortot
75018 Paris
Tel: (01) 42–78–15–18

Visits by appointment only.

Metro: Lamarck-Caulaincourt
or Pigalle
Bus: 64, 80

THE PLAQUE INDICATING SATIE'S
MONTMARTRE RESIDENCE
IS IN A SCRIPT SIMILAR TO THE
ONE USED BY THE COMPOSER.

DURING THE last decade of the nineteenth century, the French composer Erik Satie (1866–1925) lived in a room so small that he called it "a closet." Located in the hills of Montmartre, a stone's throw from the ateliers of Maurice Utrillo and his mother, Suzanne Valadon, Satie told his friends he had the feeling of being "above his creditors" and that the view outside his room extended "all the way to the Belgian frontier."

Given his wry sense of humor, Satie would probably have been delighted to know that a seven-square-meter room in the same building where he once resided has been transformed into *Le Placard d'Erik Satie* (The Closet of Erik Satie) and has been designated the "smallest museum in the world."

The museum's closet-like atmosphere is further enhanced by the dark brown cloth-covered walls and carpet. The few sticks of furniture that Satie lived with have long since disappeared. As for his two pianos, whose pedals were tied with string, these were auctioned off after his death, and purchased by Georges Braque and André Derain. Only the museum's fascinating collection of portraits, manuscripts and memorabilia offer insight into Satie's eccentric conduct and unorthodox talent.

"This museum is a symbolic dwelling," explains Ornella Volta, president of the Erik Satie Foundation, which created the museum in 1982. "Although this room is not the one he actually rented, it's an aide-mémoire of the time when he lived here."

THE TINY ONE-ROOM MUSEUM DEDICATED
TO COMPOSER ERIK SATIE,
BARELY HAS ROOM FOR A DESK, A CHAIR,
A LAMP, AND HIS ART COLLECTION.

Volta, who has studied and written extensively on Satie's life and work, says that no one really knows how the composer lived, since he never allowed anyone to visit him at home. "Despite the fact that he knew and wrote to many people, he was very solitary. You could call him a lonely extrovert," she notes.

This "lonely extrovert" made his musical debuts at the famous Montmartre cabaret, *Le Chat Noir*. Among the museum's exhibits is an

anonymous pencil portrait published
in the weekly periodical *Le Chat Noir*,
printed with the cabaret's logo. It
shows a bearded, wistful young Satie
sporting a top hat and a pince-nez.

The composer who frequented and
inspired many of this century's major
artists, including Pablo Picasso, Jean
Cocteau, Man Ray, Francis Picabia,
and Suzanne Valadon, was often
their subject as well. The museum
displays a number of portraits of
the composer, including a Pointillist
portrait by Antoine de La
Rochefoucauld, Suzanne Valadon's
superimposed charcoal profiles of a
beardless Satie and the poet J. P.
Contamine de Latour, a lithographic
proof by Pablo Picasso, and two
paintings by Augustin Grass-Mick,
one titled *Jane Avril at the Tabarin
Ball*, where Satie is portrayed next to
the dancer.

The portraits reveal the sartorial
evolution of this dandy. While the
early portraits show him with long

hair and a pince-nez that hung from a
long silk cord, later paintings, such as
the ones by Grass-Mick, portray him
in brown corduroy. During the years
he lived in his Montmartre "closet"
(1890–1898), Satie was known as the
"Velvet Gentleman" because he
favored wearing a brown velvet corduroy suit. Not wishing to be troubled to change his look, he bought
seven identical costumes, wearing out
one each year. In the twentieth century, he is portrayed in a suit complete
with English bowler, cane, and false
collar (his only personal articles of
apparel in the museum). In the
bohemian and raffish atmosphere of
Montparnasse, the composer's *petit
bourgeois* attire was all the more con-
spicuous and striking. The movie
director René Clair, who cast the
composer in his film *Entr'acte*, was so
struck by Satie's dress that he incor-
porated a likeness of the composer in
all his subsequent films.

In 1893, the highly ascetic and

solitary Satie fell in love with the painter Suzanne Valadon, who became his mistress for six months. "He felt so troubled by the relationship, that he ended it by calling in the police and telling them that Valadon was bothering him," Volta recalls, chuckling.

Still, he was never able to forget his only—albeit truncated—love affair. After his death, a packet of letters was found, addressed to Valadon but never sent, as well as a beautifully calligraphed card stating, "On the 14th of the month of January of the year of our Lord 1893, which was a Saturday, my love affair began with Suzanne Valadon, which ended on Tuesday, the 20th of the month of June of that same year."

During one of the stormiest junctures of their relationship, Satie composed a short musical piece entitled *For the Greatest Calm and the Strongest Tranquillity of my Soul*. Satie, who may go down in history as the composer of the briefest scores, wrote two lines of music for his beloved, entitled *Bon-jour Bi-qui, Bon-jour Bi-qui*. (Biqui was his pet name for Valadon.) The framed music in Satie's hand also contains the composer's quick sketch of Valadon.

When Satie wasn't sleeping or working on such compositions as *Gnossiennes* (named after the Minotaur's Labyrinth on the island of Gnossos, now Knossos), or on *Airs à faire fuir (Melodies to Make One Run Away)*, he was producing some of the wittiest hand-written notes and pamphlets of his time, some of which are part of the museum's collection.

A few months after his relationship with Valadon ended, the former Rosicrucian ceremoniously proclaimed himself the head of his own church, which he dubbed *L'Eglise Métropolitaine d'Art de Jésus Conducteur* (The Metropolitan

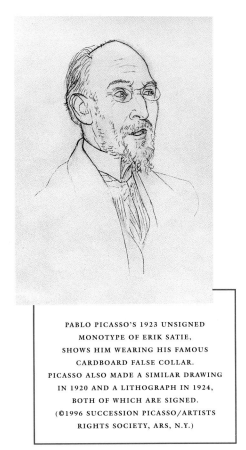

PABLO PICASSO'S 1923 UNSIGNED MONOTYPE OF ERIK SATIE, SHOWS HIM WEARING HIS FAMOUS CARDBOARD FALSE COLLAR. PICASSO ALSO MADE A SIMILAR DRAWING IN 1920 AND A LITHOGRAPH IN 1924, BOTH OF WHICH ARE SIGNED. (©1996 SUCCESSION PICASSO/ARTISTS RIGHTS SOCIETY, ARS, N.Y.)

Church of Art of Jesus the Conductor). Satie was the sole adherent of this unorthodox "church," whose headquarters were located in his "closet" at 6, Rue Cortot. Nonetheless, he claimed to have designed clerical vestments for 1,608,040,290 members, and even went so far as to issue a monthly newsletter—the *Cartulaire*—which he dispatched to various Parisian personalities.

Satie, who could spend hours contemplating the vaulting of Nôtre-Dame-de-Paris, was also enamored with Gothic lettering and Medieval French. The museum displays a pseudo-Gothic sign in Old French promoting his compositions, together with the poems of his Catalan friend, J. P. Contamine de Latour, that he hand-lettered himself and posted outside the door of his room.

In an age when poor penmanship was fashionable, Satie prided himself on his elegant script and careful calligraphy. He even made a point of saving an elegantly hand-lettered envelope, with his own personal stamp, which he mailed to himself! Now framed under glass, the envelope reads: *"Messire Erik Satie, Parcier and Master of the Chapel of the Metropolitan Church of Art."*

Although Satie shunned all artistic schools and sects—apart from his own —he clearly had a strong influence on artists who played a major role in the Dada movement, including Jean Cocteau, Francis Picabia, and Man Ray, who referred to him as "the only musician who had eyes." Not only did he write the music for such famous ballets as *Parade* and *Relâche*, but he also assembled one of the first Dada "ready-mades" with Man Ray: a steam iron stuck with a row of fourteen carpet nails, a rendition of which is also on display in the museum. (The original is at the Museum of Modern Art in New York.)

It was during the period Satie lived in Montmartre that he produced his strangest musical compositions, including one entitled *Vexations.* Published for the first time in 1969 by the musicologist Robert Caby,

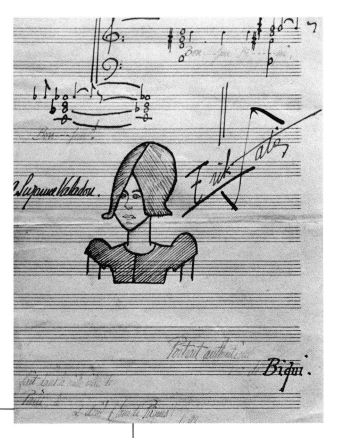

ERIK SATIE'S BRIEF MUSIC
SCORE OF *BON-JOUR BI-QUI*
WITH HIS SKETCH
OF SUZANNE VALADON.

ERTE'S ILLUSTRATION FOR *THE MONKEY IN MEDUSA'S TRAP*,
A LYRICAL COMEDY BY ERIK SATIE,
"WITH DANCE MUSIC BY THE SAME MONSIEUR, DANCED BY
A STUFFED MONKEY FROM THE MASTER'S HAND." 1974.
(COPYRIGHT SEVEN ARTS.)

along with two of the composer's other works, under the strange title *Mystical Pages*, it was recommended that the few baffling lines which make up the composition be played 840 times in a row. "It would be good to prepare oneself beforehand and in the greatest of silence through solemn immobilities," Satie advised. It is unlikely that the composer ever played this piece himself.

Three years after this closet-size museum opened, the above composition enjoyed its premiere during a European music festival, with pianist Thomas Block never leaving his clavier starting at midnight one night until midnight the next day. Now, during the annual *Fête de la Musique*, the Closet of Erik Satie hosts minute-long concerts, which long lines of auditors wait hours to hear. It's just the sort of musical performance that would have earned a round of applause from the Grand Master of the Metropolitan Church of Art, and one which he would have thoroughly appreciated.

Le Musée de la Vie Romantique

The Museum of Romantic Life

16, Rue Chaptal
75009 Paris
Tel: (01) 48-74-95-38

**Open Tuesday through Sunday
10:00 A.M. to 5:40 P.M.**

**Metro: Saint-Georges, Pigalle
Bus: 67, 74**

THE ENTRANCE TO
THE MUSEUM OF ROMANTIC LIFE,
THE FORMER RESIDENCE
OF ARTIST ARY SCHEFFER,
WHO LIVED HERE FROM 1830 UNTIL
HIS DEATH IN 1858.

In THE FALL of 1830, Louis-Philippe's court painter Ary Scheffer (1795–1858) rented a house on the Rue Chaptal (complete with servants' quarters and stables) on the edge of La Nouvelle-Athènes, a section known for its charming rural setting and affordable rents. The only thing missing was a painter's studio. Fortunately, Scheffer was able to persuade his landlord to build him two spacious ateliers where he painted, sculpted, taught, and received his artistic friends until his death in 1858.

A generous and cultivated host, Scheffer attracted the most brilliant luminaries of his day, including the painters Théodore Géricault, Gustave Moreau, Eugène Delacroix, Jean-Baptiste-Dominique Ingres, the philosopher Ernest Renan, the writer George Sand, the composers Frédéric Chopin, Franz Liszt, Gioacchino Rossini, and the opera singer Pauline Viardot. Music was such a passion with Scheffer that he invited Liszt and Chopin to play for him while he worked, sometimes accompanied by Madame Viardot. In his *Album des Peintres de l'Ecole Française*, Charles Blanc relates the memorable fusion of art and music in Scheffer's studio: "... In the midst of these finished works, canvases, and sketches, the music intensified its power and the painting seemed illuminated."

It seems a pity that this artistic and musical activity will never be reproduced in just this way again. Nonetheless, one can still have the pleasure of discovering Scheffer's lovingly restored home and garden, as well as one of his ateliers—all of which now make up the Museum of

Romantic Life in Paris's bustling ninth arrondissement.

"Visitors who walk in off the street are surprised to discover a nineteenth-century atmosphere when they come here, especially in the center of Paris. For them, it's like taking a step back into the past," notes curator Anne-Marie de Brem.

An 1851 painting by Arie J. Lamme, which provides a contemporary depiction of his cousin, Ary Scheffer, at work in his large atelier, made it feasible to faithfully recreate the original studio's interior. The spacious room, filled with light streaming in through a glass roof, has regained its brown painted walls, green shades, and ingenious sliding roof awning, as well as its main items of furniture and sculpture, including a copy of the recumbent marble effigy of his mother, Cornelia Lamme (the original of which Scheffer made for her tombstone).

Lamme's canvas, displayed in a small room abutting Scheffer's atelier, helps to conjure up a vision of how the artist worked. At the center of the painting is Scheffer, dressed in a formal black morning coat, with his back to the viewer, his right hand holding a brush, bent over his famous canvas, *L'Amour Divin, L'Amour Terrestre (Divine Love, Earthly Love)*. Scheffer's wife, Sophie Marin, whom he had married in 1850, is depicted at the rear of the studio, bent over her writing.

Ironically, even though Scheffer did much to support and encourage his peers, he himself was plagued by tremendous self-doubt regarding his own artistic abilities. In *L'Atelier d'Ary Scheffer*, curator Anne-Marie de Brem writes that critics were divided about the merits of his work. Some reviewers accused him of being deficient in draftsmanship, and of having a bland, indecisive palette devoid

THE ATELIER OF ARY SCHEFFER, RECREATED AS IT WAS WHEN THE ARTIST WAS ALIVE. ON THE WALL IS *THE ANGEL ANNOUNCING THE RESURRECTION*, THE LAST PAINTING SCHEFFER WORKED ON BEFORE HE DIED.

of brio. The most caustic criticism came from Baudelaire: after seeing Scheffer's work at the Salon of 1846, he pegged him as being *"le singe du sentiment"* ("the ape of sentiment").

Afflicted with periodic depressions throughout his life, Scheffer felt haunted by a sense of overwhelming failure, despite his many portrait commissions, a steady stream of students, and relative prosperity.

While opinions about Scheffer's paintings may still differ, two of his works are prominently displayed in the Louvre, and others are frequently included in group exhibitions. De Brem believes her museum's efforts to show the breadth and scope of Scheffer's work will help to enhance the public's knowledge of and appreciation for this artist.

Inspired by period engravings and descriptions provided by the writer's contemporaries, the museum's curatorial staff has recreated Sand's elegant yet cozy drawing room as it might have been at Nohant, the country estate where she lived and wrote. The sunny room, whose warmth is enhanced by goldenrod-colored wallpaper and rust and gold window treatment, contains the very furniture that Sand lived with at her country estate in Nohant: a Louis XV desk and armchairs, a Louis XVI chest of drawers, a writing-flap desk, a delicate pedestal table, and an embroidery frame, signs of a multifaceted woman who was as involved in the domestic as she was in her intellectual and political pursuits.

The museum's collection of sculpture, paintings, drawings, and engravings reveals how responsive Sand and her entourage were to the visual arts, as well as to the written word.

A polished plaster bust by Jean-Antoine Houdon portraying the sculptor's third daughter, Claudine (whose daughter married the sculptor Calamatta and whose grand-daughter Lina married the writer's son Maurice Sand), rests on a chest of drawers. On an easel near the fireplace is one of Sand's favorite portraits, a pastel of her great-grandfather, the Maréchal de Saxe, by Maurice-Quentin de La Tour.

Over the fireplace hangs the famous 1838 portrait of Sand with her thick mass of dark hair and penetrating gaze, presumably painted a year earlier by Auguste Charpentier, when the writer was thirty-three-years-old. A period engraving of the portrait reveals that the original canvas was rectangular and showed Sand standing next to a square-backed Flemish-style chair now in the museum's drawing-room.

The front room off the drawing-

What makes a visit to the Museum of Romantic Life so special is that— through the painstaking restoration and imaginative room settings executed by decorator Robert Garcia — a vivid impression is imparted of the life and pastimes not only of one of the nineteenth century's early Romantic painters, but also of one of its most important writers and personalities, George Sand (1804–1876), herself a long-time resident of La Nouvelle-Athènes, and a frequent guest at Scheffer's studio.

room presents a collection of portraits and personal effects belonging to Sand that evoke the writer's life and relationships. On one wall are the portraits of Alexandre Manceau, Sand's confidant and lover, Sarah Bernhardt in the role of Mariette in *François le Champi*, Ingres's drawings of the sculptor Calamatta (Maurice Sand's father-in-law), and the opera singer Pauline Viardot.

Four works by Eugène Delacroix hang on another wall. Delacroix was not only one of Sand's closest friends, but also a colleague of Scheffer's since their days as students of the Neoclassicist painter, Pierre-Narcisse Guérin.

The museum also includes a number of rare family mementos, including some of Sand's favorite jewelry, her pen and writing cases, and a dagger-shaped paper-knife that she liked to wear when she dressed as a man. One of the most moving objects is a plaster cast of Chopin's left hand with its elegant tapered fingers, executed by the sculptor Auguste Clésinger, impelling Marie Delpierre to write: "No longer and hardly any bigger than the slender, tapered hand of a woman . . . this hand, frail yet bursting with energy, expressing a liking for clarity and a sense of realism, is in itself an expression of almost all the physical and moral complexity of the artist." Next to Chopin's hand is Clésinger's plaster cast of Sand's writing arm, whose hand is distinguished by two slight malformations on the middle finger and pinky, a sign of physical strain from constant writing. It is very affecting to see these two plaster hands so tenderly reunited for posterity.

A third room decorated with teal blue wallpaper with circular designs was inspired by a small oil painting of the writer's blue bedroom in Nohant, now hanging in the same room. A small wooden pedestal table depicted in this canvas is now in the museum's drawing-room. Among the other drawings in this room are one of Sand's son Maurice as a child, dressed in the uniform of the French National Guard, and a watercolor portrait of Sand by Candide Blaize shortly after her marriage to the Baron Dudevant. Next to this portrait are the handwritten sheets of the writer's last unfinished work, *Albine*, found on her desk after she died.

Walking in the garden of the Museum of Romantic Life, with its yellow-horned poppies, purple foxglove, and non-hybrid roses, the melancholy aspects of Ary Scheffer's life are muted. His friend Delacroix wrote in his youth: "In the midst of the dull-witted, I will retreat to a temple whose walls will leave behind all that which is vulgar and flawed." The beauty, charm, and serenity of this museum and its surroundings make one feel that such yearnings may still be fulfilled.

Le Musée Zadkine

The Zadkine Museum

100 bis, Rue d'Assas
75006 Paris
Tel: (01) 43–26–91–90

Open Tuesday through Sunday
10:00 A.M. to 5:40 P.M.

Metro: Vavin, Notre-Dame-des-
Champs
Bus: 38, 58, 82, 83, 91

A FEW BLOCKS from the Luxembourg Gardens, behind an easily overlooked alley, the enterprising visitor will find the late-nineteenth-century house and ateliers where the Russian-born sculptor Ossip Zadkine (1890–1967) lived and worked from 1928 until his death. Today it has been transformed into the Zadkine Museum, thanks to a legacy from his widow, the painter Valentine Prax (1897–1981), who bequeathed her husband's entire estate to the City of Paris.

Walking through the peaceful, sculpture-filled garden, laid out virtually as Zadkine left it, one can understand why the artist chose this secluded property, an ideal spot for creating and displaying his work.

Nestled beneath the trees that he loved are many of the Cubist-

THE ENTRANCE TO THE ZADKINE MUSEUM CELEBRATES THE SCULPTOR'S DIVERSITY. (©1996 ARTISTS RIGHTS SOCIETY, ARS, N.Y./SPADEM, PARIS.)

influenced works which have established him as one of this century's most important sculptors, including *The Return of the Prodigal Son, The Residence,* and *The Water Carrier.* One of the most moving sculptures, displayed under a canopy of trees, is a legless version of *The Destroyed City,* inspired by the ruins of the bombed cities of Le Havre and Rotterdam, which Zadkine saw on his return from the United States. In 1953, a monument derived from this work, and rising 6.5 meters, was placed in Rotterdam's harbor. The arresting figure is both agonized and triumphant, an eloquent testimony to the horrors of World War II, but a tribute, as well, to the ultimate victory over Nazism.

The garden also contains the sculptor's largest version of his majestic *Orpheus,* described by many critics as Zadkine's manifesto, through which he expressed his conviction that sculpture was a poetic and lyrical art form.

In her book *Avec Zadkine, Souvenirs de Notre Vie (With Zadkine, Memories of Our Life),* Prax gives a vivid picture of the artist at work in his garden: "There in the open air, Zadkine shaped the granite and the stone of Pollinay, as well as the hardest woods. He gave the impression of being a worker, with his suit of gray velvet and his brown suede cap. He also wore big glasses to protect his eyes from the shards of wood and granite."

The presentation of the sculptor's work inside the bright and airy house and atelier is organized according to different phases of his artistic development and experimentation. "What makes Zadkine important as a sculptor is that he was constantly renewing himself," notes curator Noëlle Chabert. "Although he started out as a figurative sculptor, by the end of his life, he was moving toward abstraction. He opened the way for many abstract sculptors in the 1960s and 1970s. He was never limited by a formula."

THESE TERRA-COTTA AND BRONZE SCULPTURES WERE COMPLETED IN THE 1940S AND 1950S. (©1996 ARTISTS RIGHTS SOCIETY, ARS, N.Y./SPADEM, PARIS.)

The spare white walls, tall windows, and skylights of Zadkine's refurbished home and studio provide a handsome setting for the artist's small heads, busts, and tabletop sculptures, as well as for his larger works made of wood and bronze.

Among the most striking of Zadkine's early works, executed between 1908 and 1923, are primitive heads made either of stone or cement, reflecting the sculptor's break with academic forms. The earliest sculpture on display is a granite *Heroic Head*, reminiscent of pre-Columbian art, presumably executed while Zadkine was still in Russia.

Other works from this period illustrate the sculptor's connection to Cubism, which was to be of fundamental importance to his future development. Among the most arresting sculptures are *Feminine Shapes*, carved from lava, and *Shapes and Lights*, made of polished bronze and

noteworthy for its finely chiseled lines suggesting an eye, a lid, and a nose.

This propensity to suggest forms emerging from a mass is also evident in his imposing wooden sculpture, *The Grape Harvest*. Carved from a single block of wood, its simple forms suggest a trio of basket-laden women. Facing it on the veranda is a large, statuesque *Venus Caryatid*, her body's outlines emerging from a massive trunk of polished wood.

These works convey Zadkine's passion for carving directly into stone and wood, something that Prax recalls in her memoirs: "All his life he preferred cutting directly into stone over modeling, and he had a perfect mastery of this difficult technique. He handled his tools with great ease, as well as with great care, even making a wool casing for them to protect them from the humidity."

In the late 1920s and 1930s, Zadkine moved away from Cubist-

inspired works to a reinterpretation of classical themes, evident in the softly textured drapery of such works as *The Birth of Venus* and *The Maenads*. Although these sculptures retain certain Cubist characteristics, they also convey a sense of movement and release. *The Three Graces, Concerto,* and *Musical Trio,* all of which were sculpted in the late 1920s, demonstrate the artist's transition between his Cubist and Neoclassical periods. They also reveal one of his chief contributions to modern sculpture: whereas most sculptors of his generation produced isolated figures, he frequently portrayed groups. These figures merge with other figures, as well as with musical instruments, architectural fragments, and vegetal

LES VENDANGES (THE GRAPE HARVEST) IN WOOD (FOREGROUND) MARKS A TRANSITION BETWEEN ZADKINE'S EARLIER CUBIST PERIOD AND HIS NEOCLASSICAL PERIOD. (©1996 ARTISTS RIGHTS SOCIETY, ARS, N.Y./SPADEM, PARIS.)

forms, revealing complex harmonies of line and volume, as well as a lovely undulating rhythm.

With the fall of France, and the rise of anti-Semitism, Zadkine (who was half-Jewish) was forced to flee to the United States, where he lived, worked, and taught until 1945. (A fairly successful sculptor by this time, he had the good fortune to be on the list of European artists to whom the United States government had granted political asylum.)

Prax recalls with bitterness the pain and difficulties she underwent during this period, when she was forced to close the house and atelier on the Rue d'Assas. "With the help of the husband of my cleaning lady, I transported the bronzes into different cellars on the Rue d'Assas, and buried ten of them under coal dust." (These works were happily recovered after the war.)

Fortunately, most of Zadkine's drawings and sculptures were saved, having been hidden at the artist's country home in Arques in the Lot.

Prax was also forced to put the home and ateliers on the Rue d'Assas at the complete disposal of her tenants, who threatened to turn Zadkine's work over to the Germans if she refused. "To save his sculptures, I gave in to their demands," she recalls. (After the war, Zadkine and his wife had to sue these same tenants to regain complete possession of their home and ateliers, something that wasn't granted to the couple until 1956.)

Back in Paris, Zadkine's work underwent another metamorphosis. A row of small sculptures illustrates his struggle to bring shapes out of a foundation of disorder, an apt metaphor for post-war reconstruction. Even the titles of these works are freighted with emotion: *The Blistered Heart, The Human Forest, The Return*

LA VILLE DÉTRUITE
(THE DESTROYED CITY)
IN THE ZADKINE MUSEUM.
(©1996 ARTISTS RIGHTS SOCIETY,
ARS, N.Y./SPADEM, PARIS.)

great feeling struck a chord with his own.

In his powerful, full-length sculpture *Van Gogh Walking Through the Fields*, he portrays the haunted artist with his head shaded by a limp straw hat, his paintbox slung across his back, his notebook tucked under his arm, stalking the land like an undaunted hunter in quest of that elusive prey called Art.

The abstract sculptures in this room, the final ones Zadkine executed, reveal that capacity for self-renewal to which he was true until the end of his life. The human figure, which had been his chief source of inspiration, is absent from such late works as *Floral Shapes* and *The Cruel Door*, executed in 1967, the year of his death.

Last fall, the museum remodeled Zadkine's second atelier near the entrance and opened it for temporary expositions of the sculptor's creations, as well as the works of contemporary artists. "With the opening of this space, I hope not only to show other aspects of Zadkine's art, but also to exemplify his relevance within the context of Modernism," says curator Chabert. "By juxtaposing his work with the work of current artists, I am hoping that there will be a re-reading of his work."

Knowing Zadkine's propensity for change, this atelier seems a fitting homage to an artist who was constantly challenging his own notions of sculpture. Doubtless, it will also help attract many new admirers to this beautiful and singular museum.

of the Prodigal Son, *Incantation*, *The Dwelling*, and *Arborescence*.

Yet, at the same time as the sculptor was grappling with these broken, discontinuous forms that would culminate in his most famous work, *The Destroyed City*, he was also being drawn to the hard quality of ebony and marble and carving a number of smooth, simplified figures, such as *Pomona*, whose apple merges into her breast.

The last room in the museum is dominated by Zadkine's various likenesses of Vincent van Gogh, and the abstract works he completed at the end of his life. When the Société des Amis d'Auvers-sur-Oise commissioned a monument to the Dutch painter in 1956, Zadkine chose to approach his subject from a human angle. His aim was to capture Van Gogh the man, whose propensity for

BIBLIOGRAPHY

Anquetil, Marie Amélie.
*Musée du Prieuré, Symbolistes et Nabis,
Maurice Denis et son temps.*
Saint-Germain-en-Laye: Musée
Départemental du Prieuré, 1985.

**Bautier, Robert-Henri;
and Bautier, Anne-Marie.**
Chaalis: L'Abbaye, Les Collections.
Paris: Publications Nuit et Jour,
Beaux Arts Magazine, October 1994.

**Bayle, Luc-Marie; and Mordal,
Jacques.**
Le Musée de la Marine.
Rennes: Editions Ouest-France, 1992.

Bobot, Marie-Thérèse.
*Musée Cernuschi, Promenade dans
les Collections Chinoises.*
Paris: Editions Paris-Musées, 1983.

**Bosser, Jacques; Dering, Florian;
Gouarier, Zeev; Grodwohl, Marc;
Hook, Caroline; Jezequel,
Sandrine; Ragon, Michel; and
Weedon, Geoff.**
Art Forain.
Paris: Connaissance des Arts, 1995.

**Boudriot, Jean; Rear Admiral
Bellec, François; Burlet, René;
Demarcq, Marie-Pierre; Gay,
Jacques; Legrand, Jérôme;
Lemineur, Jean-Claude;
and Rieth, Eric.**
*Le Musée de la Marine, Palais de
Chaillot—Paris.*
Paris: Association des Amis du
Musée de la Marine, 1994.

**Cuisenier, Jean; and de Tricornot,
Marie-Chantal.**
*Musée National des Arts et Traditions
Populaires.*
Paris: Editions de la Réunion des
Musées Nationaux, 1987.

De Brem, Anne-Marie.
L'Atelier d'Ary Scheffer.
Paris: Diffusion Paris-Musées, 1991.

De Ferrière, Marc.
Christofle: 150 Ans d'Art et de Rêve.
Dijon: Dossier de l'Art, July–August
1991.

Erlande-Brandenburg, Alain.
*The Château d'Ecouen, The National
Museum of the Renaissance.*
Paris: Editions de la Réunion des
Musées Nationaux, Albin Michel,
1988.

Fäy–Hallé, Antoinette.
*Sèvres: Les Plus Riches Collections du
Monde.*
Dijon: Dossier de l'Art,
September–October 1993.

Gasc, Nadine; and Mabille, Gérard.
The Nissim de Camondo Museum.
Ghent: Artescriptum, 1991.

Lacambre, Geneviève.
*Maison d'artiste, maison-musée,
L'exemple de Gustave Moreau.*
Paris: Editions de la Réunion des
Musées Nationaux, 1987.

Lorquin, Bertrand.
Aristide Maillol.
Geneva: Editions d'Art Albert Skira
S.A., 1994.

Marchal, Henri; Bouche, Catherine; Hignette, Michel; and Noll, Colette.
Musée des Arts Africains et Océaniens.
Paris: Editions de la Réunion des Musées Nationaux, 1987.

Naffah, Christiane.
Musée de l'Institut du Monde Arabe.
Paris: Editions Pierre Anglade, 1987.

Néave, Christiane; and Charron, Hubert.
Monte-Cristo, Château de Rêve.
Marly-le-Roi: Editions Champflour, 1994.

Panati, Charles.
Extraordinary Origins of Everyday Things.
New York: Harper & Row, 1987.

Prax, Valentine
Avec Zadkine, Souvenirs de Nôtre Vie
Paris: La Bibliothèque des Arts, 1972.

Sautot, Dany.
The Story of Baccarat . . .
Paris: Baccarat, 1993.

Sérullaz, Maurice.
Delacroix.
Paris: Fayard, 1989.

Tarrit, Jean-Marc; Briot, Marie-Odile; and Jego, Bernard.
Si Montmartre m'était conté . . .
Paris: Quintessence, 1994.

Veljovic, Evelyne.
Le Musée de la Monnaie, Histoire d'un Peuple.
Paris: La Compagnie d'Hauteville, 1992.

Vierny, Dina; Lorquin, Bertrand; Daval Beran, Diane; and Daval, Jean-Luc.
Fondation Dina Vierny—Musée Maillol.
Paris: Daval Editeur S.A.

Volta, Ornella.
L'Ymagier d'Eric Satie.
Paris: Opéra de Paris—Francis Van de Velde, 1979.

INDEX

◆

Italic page numbers refer to illustrations. Because illustrations of façades, grounds, interiors, and holdings of featured museums are always located in the section devoted to the museum, museum main entries do not list illustration pages separately. Only *illustrated* works are listed by title.

Abadie, Paul, 147
Abaquesne, Masséot, 187
Abbasid dynasty, 132, 134
Abbate, Niccolo dell', 18, 22
'Abd ar-Rahman, Prince, 134
Aboriginal art, 37; *35*
Abstract art, 105, 119
Acker, François-Paul: faïence stove, *64*
Action Enchaînée, L' (Maillol), *119*
Adélaïde, Mme., 80, 82
Adélaïde of Savoy, Queen of France, 145
African art, *see* Museum of African and Oceanic Arts
Age d'Airan, L' (Rodin), *119*
Algeria, 27, 39, 41, 130
André, Edouard, 19, 20
Andrieu, Pierre, 101
Angel Announcing the Resurrection, The (Scheffer), *199*
Angers, David d': Balzac bust, 32; *32*
Anne of Austria, 114
Antoine, Jacques-Denis, 136
aquarium, 36; *36*
Arabic art, 128–35; *129, 132, 133, 135*
Architecture Studio, 128
Ardenne de Tizac, Henri d', 73
Art Deco, 36, 60
Artigues, Aimé-Gabriel d', 88
Artois, Comte d', 164
astrolabes, 134; *136*
Aubert, Jean, 18, 21
Aubert, Louis, 185
Aubrac, 52; shepherd's hut, *53*
Aubusson, 76, 164
Australia, 35, 37
automatons, 92, 93, 189; *93, 94, 190*

Baccarat, *see* Museum of Baccarat Crystal
Bahut, Mme., 100
Baigneuse Drapée ou la Seine (Maillol), *116*
Ballin, Francesco-Mogens, 105
Balzac, Bernard-François, 32–33
Balzac, Honoré de, 30–33; *32*
Balzac, Laure (Mme. Surville), 32
Bambois, Camille, 120
Bandinelli, Baccio: Medici bust, *18*
Barbarian Tribute Bearer (Chinese), 75; *71*
Barbédienne, Emile Gustave Leblanc, 72
Barrault, Jean-Louis, 173
Barre, Jacques-Jean, *139, 141*
Barrois dolls, *177*
Bauchant, André, 120
Baudelaire, Charles, 100, 101, 199
Bayol, Gustave, 45
Beaumarchais, Pierre-Auguste, 136

Beauvais tapestries, *77*
Béguin, Gilles, 73, 74
Behor, Abraham, 162, 163–64
Behor, Isaac, *see* Camondo, Isaac Behor de
Behor, Nissim, 162, 163–64; *162*
Belle Epoque, 21, 43, 111; rooms, 85; *86*
Belline (clairvoyant), 53
Belvédère, Le, see Maurice Ravel Museum
Berlioz, Hector, 148
Bernard, Emile, 108
Bernhardt, Sarah, 201
Beyle, Henri (Stendahl), 101
Bistro de l'Abreuvoir, 148
Blaize, Candide, 201
Blanc, Charles, 198
Blanche, Jacques-Emile: Dumas portrait, *24*
Block, Thomas, 197
Blum, Léon, 48
Bonaparte, Prince Louis-Napoléon, 59
Bonaparte, Princess Mathilde, 57
Bon-jour Bi-qui (Satie score), 195; *196*
Bonnard, Pierre, 105, 108, 116, 118
Bonne, Jean-Francois, 128
Boronali, Joachim-Raphael, 148
Bouchardon, Edmé, 32
Boucher, Francois, 22, 45, 80
Bouilhet, Henri, 11, 58, 59, 60
Bouilhet, Henri (great-grandfather), 59, 60
Bouilhet, Joseph, 58
Bouilhet-Christofle Museum, 11, 57–61
Boulanger, Louis, 28
Boulatov, Eric, 120
Bouquet, Louis, 36
Bourbon, Louis-Antoine de, 123
Bourdelle, Antoine: *The Grand Centaur, 107*
Bourse, 63
Bouwens, Philippe (architect), 72
Brancusi, Constantin, 119
Braque, Georges, 192
Brecker, Arno, 118
Brem, Anne-Marie de, 199
Breteuil pavilion, 63
Breton, André, 117, 157
Breugniot, Louise (Mme. de Brugnol), 31, 32
Brongniart, Alexandre, 63, 69
Brongniart, Théodore, 63
Bronze Age, The, see *Age d'Airan, L'*
Bru dolls, 176, 179; *177, 179*
Bruyr, José, 184
Buddhist art, 21, 22, 72, 74; *72, 74, 75*
Budt, Louis and Gustave de, theater of, *54*
Bullant, Jean, 187
Burne-Jones, Sir Edward Coley, 155

Cabaret des Quatre Saisons, 117
Caby, Robert, 196–97
Caesar, Julius, 51, 140
Cahen d'Anvers, Irène, 165
Calamatta (sculptor), 200, 201
Cameroon, 37, 40
Camondo, Béatrice de (Mme. Reinach), 161, 165
Camondo, Isaac Behor de, 164, 165